NATIONAL GEOGRAPHIC KiDS

Ultimate Food Atlas

Maps • Games • Recipes
for Hours of Foodie Fun

AUNT BERTHA'S FOOD TRUCK

NATIONAL GEOGRAPHIC
WASHINGTON, D.C.

TABLE OF CONTENTS

Before planning a journey, always check for alerts published by your government concerning travel to specific countries or locations. And before trying any new foods, please be aware of any food allergies you may have.

This *Ultimate Food Atlas* will take you on a fantastic food journey around the globe! Travel from continent to continent to discover a rich diversity of foods and food celebrations from many different countries. Learn about traditional meals, food attractions, cool food facts, and the food industry. Put on your chef's hat and try a few fun recipes. Foods of the world are brought to life through stunning pictures, colorful maps, and tons of fun information. This atlas also highlights sustainable eating and the ways that the world's population is fed. Get ready for a captivating around-the-world culinary adventure!

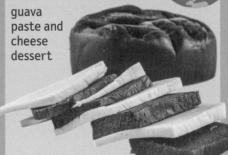
guava paste and cheese dessert

platter of cured meats with olives

 hush puppies

FOOD CATEGORIES

 Farming for Food

 Veggies, Roots, Shoots

 Fruits, Nuts, Beans, Peas

 Festivals and Feasts

 Great Grains

 Livestock and More

 Dairy Delights

 Food From the Waters

 Global Food

Global Issues

HOW TO USE THIS ATLAS

IMAGES

Images give you a taste of the foods and overall food category of each spread.

There are 195 countries in the world. Our food adventure starts in North America, but you can begin your journey on any continent you wish. Before you get started, follow Aunt Bertha's tips to experience a variety of foodie destinations.

FOOD ICON

These icons identify the food category featured on each spread.

TITLE

The book is a collection of double-page spreads. The headings and subheadings provide a summary and flavor for each spread.

INTRODUCTION

A brief introduction offers an overview of foods, ingredients, and meals grown and served on the continent.

APPETIZING ATTRACTIONS

Three interesting facts about foods grown or served at specific locations on the continent are listed and described here.

FARMING FOR FOOD

GARDENS AND HERDS

plowing the land using oxen in Ethiopia

From DATES and GRAINS to TROPICAL FRUITS

People were raising plants and animals for food in Africa more than 5,000 years ago. The ancient Egyptians, for example, grew grains, vegetables, and fruits along the Nile River. Modern African farmers generally raise a garden and a few animals. To feed the continent's growing population, individual governments and international organizations are teaching people how to grow more food on their land.

APPETIZING ATTRACTIONS

DESERT FARM
Look for rows of leafy green olive trees at the Wadi Food farm, outside Cairo, Egypt. When planting olives in the hot, dry Egyptian desert, farmers sometimes plant palm trees, too—to shade the olive trees and cool the air.

FARM SANCTUARY
At Sanctuary Farm at Lake Naivasha, Kenya, see impalas, wildebeests, zebras, and giraffes grazing alongside dairy cows. Farm owners milk their cows while also conserving their lands to protect wildlife.

SPICE UP YOUR DAY
On the island of Zanzibar off Tanzania's coast, tour a spice farm to see vanilla orchids, cinnamon, coffee, cayenne pepper, clove, and other fragrant plants—and maybe take a taste.

RECORD BREAKER
The African Rhino Horn banana plant can grow fruits up to two feet (61 cm) long! It's become popular among gardeners as an ornamental plant, and those supersize bananas are handy if you're really hungry.

92

5 COOL FOODS

1 GARDEN EGG
Uganda

Called the garden egg because of its small size and egglike shape, this crunchy fruit grows in gardens throughout Africa south of the Sahara. It comes in a variety of colors—white, red, lime green, pink, black, and even striped. Most garden eggs taste slightly bitter, but they can be eaten raw, or boiled, steamed, pickled, or added to meat and vegetable stews. The fruit is actually an eggplant, though it looks more like a tomato.

2 HUMPED CATTLE
South Sudan

What's that cow with the hump on its back? It's a zebu! Zebu cattle are well adapted to tropical countries. They were originally from Asia, and people brought them to Africa thousands of years ago. You'll recognize a zebu by the big fatty hump over its shoulders. Many zebu cattle also have a long fold of skin—called a dewlap—under their neck. Farmers in South Sudan raise zebus for their milk.

FUN FACTS

Did You Know?, Record Breaker, and Strange But True facts highlight weird, wonderful, and wacky facts about each food category.

5 COOL FOODS

These are five ingredients, dishes, meals, or drinks that will give you a flavor of the foods you can experience on each continent. Match the numbers on each picture or text block to the orange numbered circles on the map.

MAP

To find the locations mentioned on each page, check out the map. Each map also shows where land is used for crops versus pasture or production areas related to the different food categories.

DIGITAL TRAVELER

To discover even more about a country's foods, have an adult join you as you use a digital device to investigate and explore different destinations. Take photos of the amazing foods you see and taste when you travel.

RECIPES

Within each continent chapter is a Festivals and Feasts spread featuring a simple recipe for you to try. To make cooking fun and safe, never cook without an adult present. Always wash your hands with soap and warm water before and after handling food. To prevent accidents, tie up your hair, dress appropriately, take care using knives, wear mitts when handling hot food, and always turn the handles of pots and pans toward the back of the stove so people don't bump into them. When in doubt or if you have an accident, ask for help immediately.

3 MONKEY BREAD
Niger

The baobab tree grows wild in low-lying areas across Africa. In Niger, people also cultivate this valuable tree. The leaves, flowers, and roots are edible, and the fruit, sometimes called monkey bread, is used to make flour, porridge, and drinks. The name may have come from the fact that monkeys enjoy eating the fruit or that its pulp resembles bread.

4 AMARANTH
Tanzania

This leafy green vegetable grows well in East Africa's moist areas. People use the leaves for stir-fries or add them raw to salads. Some amaranth species are grown for their seeds. Boil up the amaranth seeds for a nice hot porridge for breakfast.

CONTINENT TAB

To select a continent to explore or to keep track of where you are, look at the tab on the right-hand side of each spread.

DIGITAL TRAVELER!
Peanuts, a staple crop in much of West and Central Africa, are often called groundnuts. Find out where peanuts originated—and how they differ from tree nuts such as pecans and walnuts.

FARMLAND USAGE
Pasture   Cropland
☐ Other land use

MAP GUIDE

Use the map key on each spread to interpret the different areas and symbols on the maps. For more information about maps, see pages 6–9.

5 SORGHUM
Egypt

This grain, cultivated across Africa, can be cooked like rice or popped like popcorn. It needs less water than wheat or corn. Sorghum is used in cooked dishes, salads, and snacks. Ground into flour, it is used to make pies, cookies, and bread.

93

MEASUREMENTS

In the text, measurements are given in U.S. units and then in metric units. The following abbreviations are used: C = Celsius, F = Fahrenheit, ft = feet, kg = kilograms; km = kilometers, L = liters, lb = pounds, m = meters, mi = miles, oz = ounces

AUNT BERTHA

Meet Aunt Bertha. You'll find her traveling around the world in her food truck on various pages in this book. Count how many times she appears and then check the answer key on page 150 to see if you found them all. And don't forget to read her great food travel tips!

HOW TO USE THE MAPS

M aps give visual information about the world, but you have to learn how to read them to understand what they are illustrating. The maps in this book show the shape, size, and position of continents, countries, and farming regions. They also show where on each continent different amounts of selected crops, livestock, or featured foods are grown. All the maps in this book are shown with north at the top.

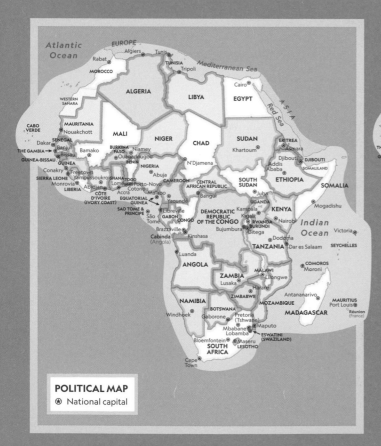

POLITICAL MAP
⊛ National capital

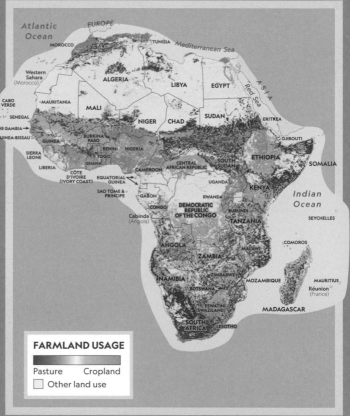

FARMLAND USAGE

Pasture   Cropland
☐ Other land use

EXPLORING CONTINENTS

The map on the first spread of each chapter is a political map of the continent. It shows country boundaries, names, and national capitals. It also shows where to find foodie hot spots featured on the spread.

FARMING THE LAND

In addition to country names and borders, the second map in each chapter shows areas where agriculture is possible on the continent. Numbers on the maps show where you can find local foods featured on the spread.

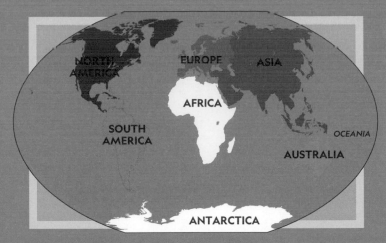

NORTH
AMERICA
EUROPE
ASIA
AFRICA
SOUTH
AMERICA
OCEANIA
AUSTRALIA
ANTARCTICA

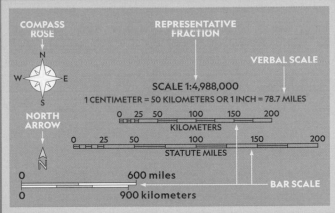

COMPASS
ROSE

REPRESENTATIVE
FRACTION

VERBAL SCALE

N
W   E
S

SCALE 1:4,988,000
1 CENTIMETER = 50 KILOMETERS OR 1 INCH = 78.7 MILES

NORTH
ARROW

0   25   50   100   150   200
KILOMETERS

0   25   50   100   150   200
STATUTE MILES

N

0   600 miles   BAR SCALE
0   900 kilometers

CONTINENTS OF THE WORLD

Earth's land area is mainly made up of seven giant landmasses known as continents. People have divided the continents into smaller political units called countries. Australia is a continent but also a single country. There is not a permanent human population on Antarctica, so for that reason it is not included in this book.

SCALE AND DIRECTION

The scale on a map may be shown as a fraction or comparison in words. A bar scale is a line or bar with measurements that compare distances on the map with those in the real world. Maps may have a compass rose or an arrow to indicate north. If north is at the top, east is to the right, west to the left, and south is at the bottom.

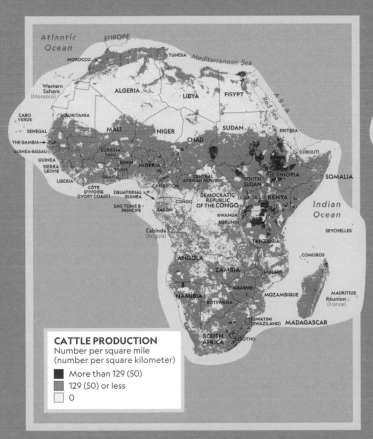

CATTLE PRODUCTION
Number per square mile
(number per square kilometer)
- More than 129 (50)
- 129 (50) or less
- 0

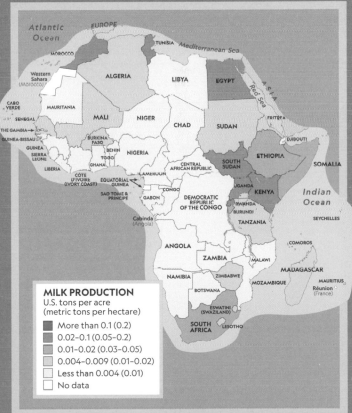

MILK PRODUCTION
U.S. tons per acre
(metric tons per hectare)
- More than 0.1 (0.2)
- 0.02–0.1 (0.05–0.2)
- 0.01–0.02 (0.03–0.05)
- 0.004–0.009 (0.01–0.02)
- Less than 0.004 (0.01)
- No data

PLANTS AND MEAT

Many types of animals are raised for food in specific areas on each continent. This map shows the number of cattle raised in these areas. Maps featuring plants grown for food show information in this same way.

MILK AND FISH

This map shows the amount of milk produced—from cattle, goats, camels, etc.—in each country on the continent. Maps showing the amount of fish caught by each country show information in this same way.

WORLD MAP

ARCTIC

Greenland
(Denmark)

ICELAND

CANADA

UNITED
KINGDOM

IRELAND

FRANCE

UNITED STATES

ATLANTIC

OCEAN

PORTUGAL   SPAIN

MOROCCO

THE
BAHAMAS

MEXICO

MAURITANIA

MALI

CUBA

DOM.
REP.

JAMAICA

ST. KITTS AND NEVIS

ANTIGUA AND BARBUDA

CABO
VERDE

BELIZE   HAITI

DOMINICA

HONDURAS

SENEGAL

BURKINA
FASO

GUATEMALA

ST. LUCIA

BARBADOS

THE GAMBIA

EL SALVADOR   NICARAGUA   GRENADA

ST. VINCENT AND THE GRENADINES

GUINEA-
BISSAU   GUINEA

GHANA

COSTA
RICA

TRINIDAD AND TOBAGO

SIERRA
LEONE

PANAMA   VENEZUELA   GUYANA

LIBERIA

COLOMBIA

SURINAME

CÔTE D'IVOIRE
(IVORY COAST)

PACIFIC   EQUATOR

ECUADOR

OCEAN

BRAZIL

PERU

SAMOA   BOLIVIA

PARAGUAY

TONGA

ATLANTIC

OCEAN

URUGUAY

CHILE

ARGENTINA

COUNTRIES OF THE WORLD

This is a political map of the world. It shows country
boundaries and country names. It also shows and
names the world's oceans.

OCEAN

RUSSIA

NORWAY
SWEDEN
FINLAND
ESTONIA
LATVIA
DENMARK
LITHUANIA
NETH.
POLAND
BELARUS
GERMANY
BELG.
LUX.
UKRAINE
SWITZ.
AUSTRIA
SLOVAKIA
MOLDOVA
CZECHIA
HUNGARY
SLOV.
ROMANIA
CRO.
ITALY
SERBIA
B.&H.
BULGARIA
GEORGIA
MONTEN.
KOSOVO
ARM.
ALBANIA
N. MACED.
GREECE
TURKEY
AZERB.
TUNISIA
MALTA
CYPRUS
SYRIA
LEBANON
ISRAEL
IRAQ
IRAN
JORDAN
KUWAIT
ALGERIA
BAHRAIN
QATAR
LIBYA
EGYPT
SAUDI
ARABIA
U.A.E.
OMAN
NIGER
YEMEN
CHAD
SUDAN
ERITREA
DJIBOUTI
NIGERIA
CENTRAL
AFRICAN
REPUBLIC
SOUTH
SUDAN
ETHIOPIA
SOMALIA
TOGO
BENIN
EQ.
GUINEA
CAMEROON
UGANDA
KENYA
SAO TOME
AND
PRINCIPE
GABON
CONGO
DEMOCRATIC
REPUBLIC
OF THE
CONGO
RWANDA
BURUNDI
TANZANIA
ANGOLA
MALAWI
COMOROS
ZAMBIA
MOZAMBIQUE
NAMIBIA
ZIMBABWE
MADAGASCAR
BOTSWANA
ESWATINI (SWAZILAND)
SOUTH
AFRICA
LESOTHO

KAZAKHSTAN
MONGOLIA
UZBEKISTAN
KYRGYZSTAN
TURKMENISTAN
TAJIKISTAN
AFGHANISTAN
PAKISTAN
CHINA
NORTH
KOREA
SOUTH
KOREA
JAPAN
NEPAL
BHUTAN
BANGLADESH
TAIWAN
INDIA
MYANMAR
(BURMA)
LAOS
THAILAND
VIETNAM
CAMBODIA
PHILIPPINES
PALAU
SRI
LANKA
MALDIVES
BRUNEI
MALAYSIA
SINGAPORE
INDONESIA
PAPUA
NEW GUINEA
TIMOR-LESTE
(EAST TIMOR)

PACIFIC
OCEAN

MARSHALL
ISLANDS
FEDERATED STATES
OF MICRONESIA
KIRIBATI
NAURU
TUVALU
SOLOMON
ISLANDS

SEYCHELLES

EQUATOR

MAURITIUS

INDIAN
OCEAN

VANUATU
FIJI

AUSTRALIA

NEW
ZEALAND

0   2000 miles
0   3000 kilometers

ANTARCTICA

NORTH AMERICA

A marvelous MENU of MEALS

North America can be thought to have six main areas. The eastern part of the continent is a mix of mountains, forests, beaches, and the sunny islands of the Caribbean Sea. At the center are the Great Plains, an expanse of flat land with grasslands and steppes. To the west are the Rocky Mountains that run north to south parallel to the Pacific coast. In the south are varied landscapes within Central America. In the southwest are dry and desert regions. In the central eastern region are the Great Lakes, the largest group of freshwater lakes in the world. The continent's diverse landscape is home to many different peoples and cultures. Combined with fertile lands for growing many foods and a melting pot of rich food traditions from all over the world, North America is a delicious place to start on our food journey!

A red barn, farmhouse, and other buildings dot a small farm in Pennsylvania, U.S.A.

FOODIE HOT SPOTS

 WHEAT GRAINS

Discover the Wheat Belt as you drive through central Canada and the midwestern U.S.

 MAPLE SYRUP

In southeastern Canada, see the majestic maple trees used to produce syrup.

 JUICY APPLES

Pick juicy apples in New York State, U.S.A., home to hundreds of apple orchards.

 A DASH OF DASHEEN

Check out the root vegetable dasheen at the Blue Food Festival on the island of Tobago.

 CORN GRAINS

In the southeastern U.S., try grits served with butter beside a morning plate of eggs.

 TASTY TACOS

Enjoy tacos al pastor—spit-roasted pork in a tortilla—at a Mexican street market.

 SAY "CHEESE"!

Visit Wisconsin, U.S.A., where cheese rules and there are more than a million dairy cows.

 SAVORY SEA SNAILS

Sample conch fritters in the Caribbean. Conchs are large, shelled marine mollusks.

 GLOBAL CORN

From the Corn Belt of the U.S.A., discover how corn is used in dishes worldwide.

FAST FACTS

Size ranking: Third largest
Number of countries: 23
Total population: 569,914,000
Largest country by area: Canada

Arctic Ocean

ASIA

Greenland
(Denmark)

Alaska
(U.S.)

Pacific Ocean

CANADA

Ottawa ✷

Atlantic Ocean

UNITED STATES

Washington,
D.C. ✷

POLITICAL MAP
✷ National capital

0   800 miles
0   800 kilometers

MEXICO

Mexico City ✷

Gulf of
Mexico

THE BAHAMAS

Nassau ✷

Havana ✷

CUBA

HAITI

**DOMINICAN
REPUBLIC**

W e s t   I n d i e s

Caribbean Sea

BELIZE
Belmopan ✷
GUATEMALA   **HONDURAS**
Guatemala City ✷   Tegucigalpa ✷
San Salvador ✷   **NICARAGUA**
EL SALVADOR   Managua ✷
San José ✷   Panama
   City ✷
COSTA RICA   **PANAMA**

AREA ENLARGED BELOW

SOUTH AMERICA

AUNT BERTHA'S FOOD TRAVEL TIPS

* Summer in North America is the time to visit outdoor fairs and festivals to try regional foods. Step up to a booth and try something new, like fried cheese curds in Wisconsin, buckeye candy in Ohio, or poutine in Canada.

* Discover the many farmers markets selling goods around North America. Markets give you the opportunity to meet farmers and other food producers and experience where the locals shop for their food.

* Along the coasts, stroll down to the docks and watch fishing boats return with their catches. You might be able to have a seaside bite.

CUBA

Cayman
Islands
(U.K.)

JAMAICA

HAITI

Port au
Prince ✷   Santo
   Domingo ✷
Kingston ✷

**DOMINICAN
REPUBLIC**

Virgin Islands
(U.S.)   (U.K.)

Puerto Rico
(U.S.)

Basseterre ✷

**ST. KITTS
& NEVIS**

✷ St. John's

ANTIGUA & BARBUDA

Caribbean Sea

DOMINICA
Roseau
Castries ✷

ST. LUCIA
Kingstown ✷

BARBADOS
Bridgetown ✷

Aruba
(Neth.)

Curaçao
(Neth.)

**ST. VINCENT &
THE GRENADINES**
GRENADA ✷ St. George's

Bonaire
(Neth.)

TRINIDAD & TOBAGO
Port of Spain ✷

0   400 miles
0   400 kilometers

SOUTH AMERICA

A SUPER SELECTION

oranges ready for picking in California, U.S.A.

FAB FOODS from COAST to COAST

North America's diverse habitats and broad range of temperatures make it an ideal place to grow, catch, and harvest a huge selection of foods. Vast, flat lands in the midwestern United States and southern Canada are perfect for dairy farming and growing wheat and corn. Warmer temperatures in the south provide the right conditions for citrus groves. In Central America and the Caribbean islands, tropical fruits are common. Throughout North America, you'll find fields, orchards, ranches, and farms to suit every appetite. Canada's cool, crisp waters are the perfect home for salmon to run and spawn and for mussels to be farmed.

? DID YOU KNOW?

Salty, citrusy, crunchy chapulines, or crickets, are a highly nutritious treat and a great source of protein dating back to before the Spanish introduced domesticated animals to Mexico. As a snack, they are baked with tomatillos and herbs, sprinkled with salt and drops of lime juice, and served in tortillas.

5 COOL FOODS

 **APPETIZING ATTRACTIONS**

➤ LIVING-HISTORY FARMS
Visit simulated historical farms in Urbandale, Iowa, to learn and experience how farming has developed in the United States since the 1700s. Iowa produces more corn than any other state in the country.

➤ AVOCADOS APLENTY
Visit the state of Michoacán in Mexico, where you can find more than 30,000 avocado orchards. Trees bloom throughout the year, and pulp from the fruits is eaten raw and used to make dips and soups.

➤ COWBOYS AND CUISINE
Saddle up and get to the Calgary Stampede, an annual rodeo, agricultural exhibition, and food festival in Calgary, Alberta, Canada. The stampede takes place in July, but the venue runs year-round events related to farming and food.

1 ENCHILADAS CON MOLE
Mexico

Often served with a sauce that dates back to Maya times, enchiladas are popular throughout Mexico. They are corn wraps filled with cheese, beans, vegetables, or meat. There are many varieties of sauces that go on top, but one of the most unique is mole from Oaxaca. Pronounced *MOH-lay*, it is made from chili peppers, nuts, onions, spices, and chocolate.

2 TOURTIÈRE
Canada

This French-Canadian flaky meat pie is a must on every holiday plate in Québec City. It dates back to the early French settlers of the 1600s.

DIGITAL TRAVELER!
Caribbean foods are inspired by African, Creole, Cajun, East Indian, Chinese, and European cuisines. If you're visiting a Caribbean island, search for dishes you can try.

Arctic Ocean

ASIA

Greenland (Denmark)

Alaska (U.S.)

Pacific Ocean

3 MOFONGO
Puerto Rico

Plantains are the main ingredient in this Puerto Rican staple. The plantains are picked green, fried, then mashed with garlic, salt, and oil until they resemble mashed potatoes. Puerto Ricans add pork cracklings called chicharrón to turn this into an extra-tasty side dish for grilled fish or another main course.

CANADA

FARMLAND USAGE
Pasture — Cropland
Other land use

UNITED STATES

Atlantic Ocean

4 GUMBO
United States

Try a bowl of this rich vegetable and meat or shellfish stew with West African and French origins for an authentic taste of New Orleans. Like North America itself, this stew is truly a tasty melting pot of flavors.

THE BAHAMAS

West Indies

Gulf of Mexico

CUBA

MEXICO

HAITI

Puerto Rico (U.S.)

Caribbean Sea

BELIZE   HONDURAS

GUATEMALA
EL SALVADOR

NICARAGUA

SOUTH AMERICA

COSTA RICA

PANAMA

5 MIXTO
Cuba

This popular Cuban sandwich consists of lightly buttered Cuban bread filled with sliced pork, thinly sliced ham, Swiss cheese, dill pickles, and mustard.

5 COOL FOODS

1 CARROTS
Canada

Roasted with maple syrup, baked in a cake, steamed, or eaten raw, carrots are popular in Canada. Ontario is the number one carrot growing province in the country, and the city of Bradford, Ontario, even has a carrot as its mascot.

DID YOU KNOW?

It takes about 50 gallons (189 L) of maple sap to produce one gallon (3.8 L) of maple syrup. A typical maple tree produces between 10 and 20 gallons (38–76 L) of sap each year.

2 POTATOES
United States

French fries made from Idaho potatoes can be found in restaurants across the United States. This vegetable originated in South America and is now a staple throughout the Americas. It is eaten baked, fried, boiled, whole, sliced, or mashed.

3 CALLALOO
Caribbean

Made from coconut milk and the leafy greens of taro or amaranth, this vegetable stew adds a richness to meals from Jamaica, Dominica, and other Caribbean islands.

Arctic Ocean

ASIA

Greenland (Denmark)

Alaska (U.S.)

CANADA

Pacific Ocean

Atlantic Ocean

UNITED STATES

ROOTS and TUBERS PRODUCTION*
U.S. tons per acre (metric tons per hectare)

- ■ More than 5.7 (12.7)
- ■ 5.7 (12.7) or less
- □ 0

*Not all roots and tubers shown

THE BAHAMAS

West Indies

Gulf of Mexico

MEXICO

CUBA

HAITI DOMINICAN REPUBLIC

Caribbean Sea

BELIZE HONDURAS

GUATEMALA
EL SALVADOR

NICARAGUA

SOUTH AMERICA

COSTA RICA

PANAMA

pancakes and maple syrup

A VARIETY OF VEGGIES

From CACTUS FRIES to MAPLE SYRUP

From wild forests to cultivated farms, a feast of nature's textures and tastes comes from root, shoot, and leaf crops grown in North America. The plants sweeten our world, fill our bellies, and nourish our bodies. They include sugar maple trees growing in deciduous forests in the northeastern United States and Canada, cactus leaves in Mexico, and sugar cane on Caribbean islands. Soft, fleshy, nutritious plant parts include tubers, rhizomes, corms, bulbs, roots and stems, and sprays of fine leaves. As potatoes, lettuces, carrots, herbs, and more, they are served at many North American meals. Mushrooms—a type of fungi—are also used as an ingredient in some dishes, mainly in the United States and Canada.

APPETIZING ATTRACTIONS

FOOD CART FEAST

In Portland, Oregon, in the northwestern United States, more than 600 tiny kitchens serve all kinds of vegetables and other dishes at food cart communities known as pods. The pods are found around the city.

VEGETABLE MARKET

Pick up some fresh cabbages, turnips, and other vegetables from one of 130 local sellers at this weekly Saturday market in Old Strathcona, Edmonton, Canada. The market's motto is, "We make it, we bake it, we grow it, and we sell it."

BOTANIC GARDENS

Visit Deshaies Botanical Gardens on the Caribbean island of Guadeloupe to see many of the tropical North American plants that produce roots, shoots, and leaves that we eat. Ask a guide to explain how the plants grow.

4 CACTUS FRIES
Mexico

Enjoy these tasty fries made from the prickly pear cactus when visiting the Sonoran Desert, found in Mexico and the southwestern United States. After the needles are removed, segments of the cactus are sliced, battered, and deep fried.

5 RHUBARB
United States

This greenish red stalk is picked in spring, chopped up, and added to pies and jams. In the eastern United States, a strawberry-rhubarb pie is a favorite dessert in early summer. But never eat the leaves of this plant. They're poisonous!

DIGITAL TRAVELER

Many sweeteners—like maple syrup, sugar cane, and agave—come from plants. Grab an adult and search online for other natural food sweeteners. Which come from North America?

PLUCKED FROM THE EARTH

BERRY pies, bean stews, and MORE

Citrus zests, fields of sun-ripened tomatoes, and bogs of floating cranberries can be found in the different temperature zones of North America. Some fruits, such as oranges and lemons, need hot, sunny climates. Others, like blueberries, grow better in cooler, moister areas, like the U.S. state of Maine. North America has all kinds of fruits, from berries, melons, and stone fruits to pineapples, avocados, and limes. Legumes, including peas and beans, also grow here. Pigeon peas and kidney beans grow in tropical gardens on Caribbean islands and on parts of the mainland. With such a huge variety of ingredients, there are lots of tasty dishes to try.

tomatoes

DID YOU KNOW?

Tomatoes are a fruit that originated in the Americas. Italian tomato sauce wasn't created until long after the fruit was brought to Italy in the 16th century. The British didn't embrace tomatoes until much later, fearing they were poisonous. The leaves, roots, and stems of tomato plants are mildly toxic if eaten.

5 COOL FOODS

DIGITAL TRAVELER!

The fragrant pods of vanilla orchids create a flavor used in cakes, ice cream, and root beer. Grab an adult and go online to find out how vanilla pods are harvested and processed to make natural vanilla extract.

1 KEY LIMES
United States

Oranges and grapefruits aren't the only citrus fruits grown in Florida. Key limes are famously used in tasty tart pies sold in stores and at roadside stands in the Florida Keys.

2 RASPBERRY CHEESECAKE
Canada

Is it a pie or is it a cheesecake? It's both! Prince Edward Island, Canada, boasts tasty raspberry cheesecake pies made with the island's rich raspberries. The pie makes a perfect summertime dessert to share.

Greenland
(Denmark)

ASIA

Alaska
(U.S.)

Arctic Ocean

CRANBERRY BOG TOUR

In Wareham, Massachusetts, U.S.A., near Cape Cod, visit the A.D. Makepeace Company for a bog tour and to learn how cranberries are grown and how most berries are processed for juice.

PICK YOUR OWN STRAWBERRIES

Strawberries can be harvested from spring into fall. La Fruiterie Champêtre is a pick-your-own farm in Québec, Canada, where you can fill your basket with fruit to make strawberry shortcake, a popular dessert there.

MANGO MADNESS

Visit the Caribbean in the summer and you'll find fresh mangoes and mango dishes sold in markets and street stalls. Pick, eat, and share these tasty fruits on St. Lucia and other islands.

FRUIT PRODUCTION*
U.S. tons per acre
(metric tons per hectare)

- More than 10.7 (24)
- 10.7 (24) or less
- 0

*Not all fruits shown

CANADA

UNITED STATES

Atlantic Ocean

Gulf of Mexico

MEXICO

GUATEMALA
EL SALVADOR

BELIZE
HONDURAS
NICARAGUA
COSTA RICA
PANAMA

West Indies

THE BAHAMAS

CUBA
HAITI
DOMINICAN REPUBLIC

Caribbean Sea

SOUTH AMERICA

5 PEAS AND RICE
The Bahamas

No matter what you order, you'll probably find a side of peas and rice beside your Bahamian meal. It's chock-full of delicious red or green pigeon peas and rice seasoned with tomatoes, onions, and pork.

3 APPLE PIE
United States

When fall apples are ripe, it is time to slice them up, add some cinnamon and sugar, and place them in a pie crust to make apple pie. Bake one yourself or pick one up at a market. If you're near San Diego, California, U.S.A., you can try an apple pie at any time of year at the Julian Pie Company, whose motto is "As American as Apple Pie."

4 FRIJOLES REFRITOS
Mexico

Frijoles refritos are fried mashed beans. They are a yummy staple beside Mexican main dishes. Traditionally, pinto beans are used. When stewed with onion, garlic, and bacon, pinto beans make a dish called frijoles charros, or cowboy beans!

TASTY DAYS

Cinco de Mayo festival in Durango, Colorado, U.S.A.

FUN TIMES and tempting TASTES

Food festivals and fairs are usually full of cooking competitions, eating contests, and tons of new ways to enjoy the main attraction—food! They are great opportunities to sample national dishes, indigenous ingredients, and novel ways of preparing and presenting meals. Check out these fantastic harvest and community foodie festivals celebrated in different areas of North America at various times each year.

DIGITAL TRAVELER!
Orotina, in the country of Costa Rica, is known as the "City of Fruits." Each March, it hosts a fruit festival, complete with a horse parade and dancing. Find out which tropical fruits you can sample here.

1 BLUE FOOD FESTIVAL
Trinidad and Tobago

Every October for more than 20 years, the residents of Bloody Bay, Tobago, have celebrated the ingredient dasheen, a relative of taro that thrives on the island. On Tobago, dasheen is usually served boiled as a side dish, or cut up and used in soups or vegetable dishes. When cooked, some varieties of dasheen turn a blue color, hence the festival's name.

2 THANKSGIVING
United States

This historical holiday held every November is a time to give thanks and share a bountiful meal with family. It has its roots in colonial America. The traditional dinner includes turkey, stuffing, and many vegetable side dishes. Each family fills the Thanksgiving table with its own favorite cultural dishes. Canada celebrates its own Thanksgiving each October.

3 POUTINEFEST
Canada

Every May, Ottawa is the place to get your fill of Canada's celebrated cheesy, gravy-doused fries. At PoutineFest, different types of sauces are used as well as gravy, and the fries are often served with sausages, smoked meats, chicken, and even truffles.

1. Trinidad and Tobago
2. United States
3. Canada
4. Mexico
5. United States

NORTH AMERICA

4 CORN AND TORTILLA FAIR
Mexico

Each May, people of Santiago Tepalcatlalpan, Mexico, celebrate their staple crop, corn. Try tlacoyos, which are cakes of corn dough stuffed with beans, a honey-cornmeal candy called ponteduros, or grilled corn flavored with chili and cheese.

5 HUDSON VALLEY GARLIC FESTIVAL
United States

Sample everything from garlicky shrimp scampi to garlic-flavored ice cream at this annual fall festival—which celebrates the harvest of this "stinking rose"—in New York State's Hudson Valley.

TRY THIS RECIPE
POUTINE SAUCE
A TASTE OF CANADA

Poutine is a classic Canadian dish that includes french fries, cheese curds, and a brown gravy, or sauce. If you can't find cheese curds, chunks of full-fat mozzarella cheese can be used instead.

Prep time: 30 minutes for the sauce
Serves: 3 people

3 tablespoons cornstarch
2 tablespoons water
6 tablespoons butter
¼ cup all-purpose flour
2½ cups beef broth
1¼ cups chicken broth
salt to taste
black pepper to taste
white cheddar cheese curds or torn chunks of
    full-fat mozzarella cheese for topping

1. In a small bowl, combine the cornstarch and water and stir until fully dissolved. Set aside.
2. With an adult's help, melt the butter in a large saucepan over medium-high heat. Add the flour, stirring often until the mixture is smooth and golden brown.
3. With an adult's help, carefully pour both broths into the pan. Stir with a whisk and bring the mixture to a boil.
4. Stir in the cornstarch and water mixture. Lower the heat and simmer the sauce for 10 to 20 minutes until it thickens. Stir often.
5. Add salt and pepper to taste. Serve poutine sauce over fries, and top with cheese curds or torn chunks of mozzarella. Serve hot.

CEREALS AND MORE

From BAGELS to BEAVERTAILS

a bowl of oatmeal

Grains are the small dried seeds of plants grown and harvested for food. Most important are cereal grains, including corn, wheat, barley, rye, oats, rice, and millet. Other types include buckwheat and quinoa. North American pantries are filled with all kinds of grains. Sometimes, they are ground to make products like cornmeal and multigrain flour. Other times, they're processed into pancake batters, cake mixes, and breakfast cereals. And don't forget the whole grains, because people eat a lot of those, too. Grains of all kinds are a major part of many people's diets in North America.

APPETIZING ATTRACTIONS

MITCHELL CORN PALACE
Join more than 500,000 visitors each year at this historic, one-of-a-kind attraction in Mitchell, South Dakota, U.S.A. The palace is decorated with murals made from corn and other grains in many different natural colors.

READING TERMINAL MARKET
Visit one of America's oldest public markets in Philadelphia, Pennsylvania, U.S.A., and find freshly made Amish doughnuts, locally made cheeses, famous Philly cheesesteaks, and oodles of grain products, meats, and seafood. It's the perfect spot to find a new favorite food or to buy ingredients to create your own foodie masterpiece.

PASTRY PASSIONS
In Kingston, Jamaica, visit a Pastry Passions bakery outlet to sample a wide variety of Caribbean cakes and pastries made from family recipes.

5 COOL FOODS

1 HUSH PUPPIES
United States

Try these fried balls of cornmeal that, according to legend, were once given to barking puppies to hush them. Now often served with honey butter, you can enjoy them as a favorite side with meals in the southern United States.

2 BAGELS
United States

Bagels are a favorite lunch and breakfast item. Often spread with cream cheese, the classic New York–style bagel is made from yeasted dough that is cut, rolled, formed into rings, and then boiled before being baked. With or without cream cheese, bagels are often topped with sliced smoked fish, meat, or eggs.

3 BEAVERTAILS
Canada

First made in Ontario but now found across Canada, these fried pastries are made from Canadian wheat. The dough is hand-stretched to form the shape of a beaver's tail. Each beavertail is topped with cinnamon and sugar, sliced bananas, hazelnut cream, or whipped cream.

4 TORTILLAS
Mexico

This flatbread can be made from either corn or wheat. Try using a tortilla as an eating utensil as is done in Mexico. To make a taco, a corn or flour tortilla is folded in half around a filling. Burritos are usually made with flour tortillas, which are rolled around fillings that include beans, rice, meat, or eggs. Fajitas are strips of meat or chicken served with flour tortillas on the side.

DIGITAL TRAVELER!
Fry bread, a bread eaten by Native Americans, was named South Dakota's state bread in 2005. Discover the origins of this historical food.

GRAIN PRODUCTION*
U.S. tons per acre
(metric tons per hectare)

- More than 0.1 (0.3)
- 0.1 (0.3) or less
- 0

*Not all grains shown

5 ATOLE
Guatemala

This warm, milky corn drink is usually served at breakfast and seasoned with cinnamon or vanilla. Wholesome and nutritious, it is almost a meal on its own. In Guatemala and other Central American countries, atole is widely available in cafés.

Map labels:
Arctic Ocean
ASIA
Alaska (U.S.)
Greenland (Denmark)
CANADA
UNITED STATES
Atlantic Ocean
MEXICO
Gulf of Mexico
THE BAHAMAS
West Indies
CUBA
HAITI
DOMINICAN REPUBLIC
Caribbean Sea
BELIZE HONDURAS
Pacific Ocean
GUATEMALA
EL SALVADOR
NICARAGUA
COSTA RICA
PANAMA
SOUTH AMERICA

DID YOU KNOW?
Wheat was the first cereal plant that people grew and harvested for food. Evidence from the Middle East shows that people cultivated wheat grains around 8000 B.C. Cereal plants were first cultivated in North America around 5000 B.C. near present-day Mexico City.

2 CANADIAN BACON
Canada

Canadian bacon comes from the loin of the pig, where pork chops come from. The meat isn't smoked, but instead is pickle-cured and rolled in fine cornmeal. Slices of Canadian bacon go well with a plate of eggs.

5 COOL FOODS

1 HAMBURGER
United States

Americans are said to eat more than 50 billion burgers each year, enough to circle Earth 32 times. To sample this meat-in-a-bun meal, grab a burger from a fast-food restaurant or make your own at home. Spice it up with mustard, ketchup, or another favorite topping.

3 BARBECUE
United States

Barbecue is a traditional way of cooking meat, fish, or vegetables in wood smoke over an open pit. Sample barbecue pork ribs, beef brisket, or pulled pork in Texas, Missouri, Tennessee, or North Carolina and join the debate over which state cooks it the best. The preparation is different in each locale, giving each variety a unique smoky flavor. Wherever you eat BBQ, you'll find it finger-licking good.

Arctic Ocean

ASIA

Greenland
(Denmark)

Alaska
(U.S.)

Atlantic
Ocean

CANADA

2

UNITED STATES

1

CATTLE PRODUCTION
Number per square mile
(number per square kilometer)

■ More than 129 (50)
■ 129 (50) or less
□ 0

3

THE
BAHAMAS

West Indies

MEXICO

Gulf of
Mexico

CUBA

JAMAICA

HAITI DOMINICAN
REPUBLIC

Caribbean Sea

Pacific
Ocean

4

BELIZE

HONDURAS

5

GUATEMALA
EL SALVADOR

NICARAGUA

SOUTH AMERICA

COSTA RICA

PANAMA

LIVESTOCK AND MORE

A WIDE VARIETY

a breakfast of bacon and eggs

From FAST FOODS to FASCINATING dishes

North Americans are known for eating a great deal of meat and eggs. In fact, far more land on this continent is used for grazing livestock than for growing fruits and vegetables. North America is home to huge cattle ranches and poultry farms as well as lots of smaller family farms. These operations—both conventional and free-range—raise everything from cows and pigs to chickens and turkeys. This offers chefs and diners a huge variety of foods to choose from. So how do you like your meat and eggs cooked? Whatever your preference, you can find it here!

DIGITAL TRAVELER!
Surf the web with an adult to find the latest winners of the popular Nathan's Famous Hot Dog Eating Contest, which is held in New York City each summer.

APPETIZING ATTRACTIONS

↪ THREE BARS DUDE RANCH
Experience a working cattle ranch in the Rocky Mountains of British Columbia, Canada. Programs for kids offer cooking food over an open fire and horseback riding.

↪ LAMAR BUFFALO RANCH
In Yellowstone National Park, U.S.A., visit the historic corrals that helped save the buffalo—more correctly, the bison—from extinction—and also brought this big-hoofed mammal to the American table.

↪ HOME COOKING
Visit small, family-run restaurants in Mexico City called fondas for a great breakfast of Mexican-style eggs served with sauce. You might even want to order escamoles, which are small, fried, egg-shaped ant pupae!

4 TACOS AL PASTOR
Mexico

In Puebla, try one of Mexico's most common foods, tacos al pastor. This popular meat wrap was created in the 1930s by Lebanese immigrants to the city and involves cooking pork on a spit.

5 JERK CHICKEN
Jamaica

Try this tasty island chicken that has been hand-rubbed with spices. The term "jerk" comes from the action of poking holes in the cooking chicken, which helps the meat absorb the spicy flavors.

STRANGE BUT TRUE
It is believed that pigs were introduced to North America in 1493, when Christopher Columbus brought them by ship from Spain to Cuba.

23

MADE FROM MILK

From CREAMY to CRUMBLY

Explore nutrient-rich milk and dairy foods all across North America. From Holstein and Jersey cows to Nubian and LaMancha goats, livestock can be found throughout the continent. Milk from these animals is used to produce many varieties of cheese, yogurt, milk, and sour cream. Farms range from small, organic family farms that sometimes offer tastings, to large commercial dairy operations. North Americans don't have to go far for locally made ice cream in the summer or to get the cheese that fills the warm grilled cheese sandwiches they eat year-round.

grilled cheese sandwiches

ASIA

Alaska (U.S.)

Pacific Ocean

5 COOL FOODS

2 ICE CREAM
Canada

Try a locally made ice cream anywhere in North America. If you are in Canada, head to Slickers in Bloomfield, Ontario. Its unique flavors include toasted marshmallow, apple pie, and passion fruit.

1 PASTEL DE TRES LECHES
Nicaragua

This sweet and tasty cake, said to have originated in Nicaragua, is made from three kinds of milk—whole, sweetened condensed, and evaporated. The result is a creamy, moist vanilla cake that is the perfect ending to any meal. It is usually served with a topping of vanilla whipped cream.

3 QUESO FRESCO
Mexico

Often made with a mixture of goat's and cow's milk, this soft white cheese can be crumbled on top of tacos or grilled corn. Its name, in Spanish, means "fresh cheese."

4 FLAN
Honduras

Dip your spoon into this sweet caramelized custard made from eggs and cream. Originally brought to the New World from Spain, it is eaten on its own or served with fruit.

APPETIZING ATTRACTIONS

MILKSHAKE MARKET
Cayo is a culinary hot spot in Belize. Visit a market in Placencia and try some local foods, including a delicious seaweed shake. Made with milk, blended seaweed, and a mix of spices, it is a refreshing drink.

ICE-CREAM FACTORY TOUR
Visit the Ben & Jerry's ice-cream factory in Waterbury, Vermont, U.S.A., to sample lots of unique flavors.

CHEESE TRAILS
Follow an organized cheese trail across Ontario and British Columbia to tour top cheesemakers in Canada. You can taste samples at each place you visit.

MILK PRODUCTION
U.S. tons per acre
(metric tons per hectare)

■	More than 0.1 (0.2)
■	0.02–0.1 (0.05–0.2)
■	0.01–0.02 (0.03–0.05)
■	0.004–0.009 (0.01–0.02)
□	Less than 0.004 (0.01)
□	No data

Arctic Ocean

Greenland (Denmark)

CANADA

UNITED STATES

Atlantic Ocean

MEXICO

Gulf of Mexico

THE BAHAMAS

West Indies

CUBA

HAITI DOMINICAN REPUBLIC

Caribbean Sea

BELIZE HONDURAS

NICARAGUA

GUATEMALA
EL SALVADOR

COSTA RICA

PANAMA

SOUTH AMERICA

5 YOGURT
United States

You can find yogurt made from the milk of different animals (cows, goats, or sheep) and in different styles (traditional, Greek, Icelandic, or a rich Australian-style variety) on grocery store shelves throughout the country.

STRANGE BUT TRUE
More than 17,000 cows are milked each day to make Hershey's milk chocolate.

DIGITAL TRAVELER!
Cheese experts come to U.S. cities from all over the world for the annual Cheesemonger Invitationals. With an adult's help, go online to find details on events, locations, and previous winners.

a North American seafood platter

FOOD FROM THE WATERS

FRESHLY CAUGHT

From SHELLFISH to FLYING FISH

North American waters, both freshwater and saltwater, are filled with foods you can eat—everything from shrimp and salmon to trout, mussels, and crawfish. All along the North Atlantic and Pacific coasts and around the Caribbean islands, fishing vessels bring their sea catches to shore. Many fish and shellfish are also raised and harvested in coastal fish farms, and freshwater fish and shellfish are harvested from lakes and rivers, too. Whether you're craving seaweed dishes in Belize or crawfish boils in Louisiana, U.S.A., the waters in and around North America have everything you need to create a delicious meal.

APPETIZING ATTRACTIONS

➤ FISHERMAN'S WHARF

Enjoy steamy clam chowder in a sourdough bread bowl as you watch fishers arrive with their catch at this historic port in San Francisco, California, U.S.A.

➤ ARAWAK CAY FISH FRY

Have an authentic Bahamian fish fry just 10 minutes from downtown Nassau at this seaside attraction. You can taste seafood island treats, from conch salads to fish that is battered, deep-fried, and served with calypso sauce.

➤ PEGGY'S COVE

The famous Peggy's Cove Lighthouse might draw the crowds, but people stay for the seafood in this famous Nova Scotia fishing town. Try the fish-and-chips, seafood chowder, or lobster tail thermidor.

5 COOL FOODS

1 MUSSELS
Canada

Prince Edward Island in Canada is famous for its mussels, usually eaten steamed with melted butter. You can eat them right out of the pot. Mussels are also used in chowders, which are thick soups or stews made with all kinds of seafood and vegetables.

RECORD BREAKER

To celebrate New Orleans' 300th anniversary in 2018, a record 300-foot (91.4-m)-long po'boy sandwich was made with 175 pounds (79.4 kg) of shrimp filling.

Arctic Ocean

ASIA

Alaska (U.S.)

Greenland (Denmark)

2 CRAWFISH BOIL
United States

Crawfish, the official state crustacean of Louisiana, resemble tiny lobsters and are found in creeks and in wetlands known as bayous. Feast like the Cajuns—local people of French descent— with a crawfish boil that includes corn, potatoes, onions, garlic, and plenty of crawfish.

5 FLYING FISH
Barbados

Steamed or fried and served up with butter, tomatoes, and fresh herbs, flying fish is the national dish of Barbados. You'll even see its picture on the country's currency. Try it at a local café or restaurant.

3 CETI
Puerto Rico

In Arecibo, Puerto Rico, ceti are a local delicacy. These tiny fish, caught in the local sea from July through December, are cooked and eaten whole. Sometimes they are wrapped into an empanada, a baked or fried pastry turnover.

4 BAJA FISH TACO
Mexico

Near the seaside in Baja California, try this taco with freshly caught whitefish, a pickled slaw called curtido, and a squeeze of lime—all wrapped in a delicious corn tortilla.

AMOUNT OF FISH CAUGHT
Average pounds (kilograms) per person per year

- More than 132 (60)
- 68–132 (31–60)
- 46–67 (21–30)
- 11–45 (5–20)
- Less than 11 (5)

CANADA

UNITED STATES

Atlantic Ocean

Gulf of Mexico

MEXICO

Pacific Ocean

West Indies

BAHAMAS

CUBA

HAITI

Puerto Rico (U.S.)

Caribbean Sea

BARBADOS

BELIZE

GUATEMALA

EL SALVADOR

HONDURAS

NICARAGUA

COSTA RICA

PANAMA

SOUTH AMERICA

VITAL CORN

cobs of flint corn

A MULTIPURPOSE food STAPLE

Although some people call it corn and others call it maize, corn on the cob is a familiar—and delicious—summer treat around the world. Corn is also a staple grain in many cultures, as it can be stored easily and eaten throughout the year. To the ancient Maya and their descendants who still live where corn originated in the Americas, "maize is life."

There are six varieties of corn—dent, flint, pod, popcorn, flour, and sweet—and there are many subvarieties within each category. Kernels can be red, blue, purple, white, yellow, or multicolored. Corn can be cooked in many different ways or eaten raw right off the cob. People in some cultures add spices to their corn. Others add cheese, ice cream, or soy sauce. Corn has been introduced to countries throughout the world and is found in drinks, breads, soups, and desserts.

TRUE OR FALSE?

Which of these statements about corn are true and which are false?

1. Corn is used to make biofuel to power cars.
2. People eat most of the corn grown in the United States.
3. Corn mazes are popular springtime tourist attractions on farms.
4. You can drink your corn in the form of a juice in Peru.
5. Popcorn is not really made from corn.

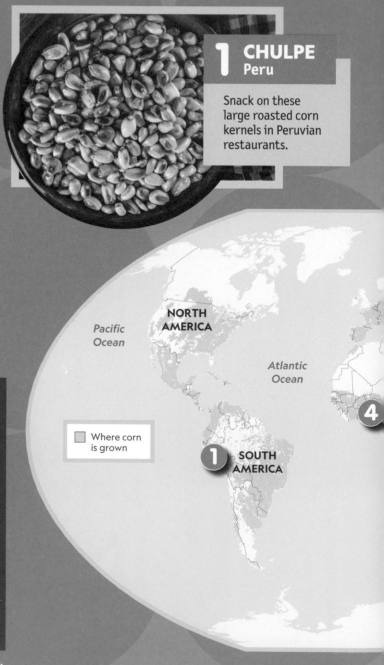

5 COOL FOODS

1 CHULPE Peru

Snack on these large roasted corn kernels in Peruvian restaurants.

NORTH AMERICA

Pacific Ocean

Atlantic Ocean

Where corn is grown

1 SOUTH AMERICA

4

See answers on page 150.

2 POLENTA
Italy

Taste this specialty of ground flint corn or wheat as a side dish in food outlets in northern Italy. Sometimes polenta is served like a creamy porridge, and sometimes it is grilled with toppings.

3 MAKKI DI ROTI
India

Taste this unleavened bread made from corn or wheat in the Punjab region of India and Pakistan. It is usually eaten warm with cooked vegetables or curries.

4 UKPO OKA
Nigeria

This steamed corn pudding from the Niger Delta is often wrapped in leaves to give it an earthy flavor. It is also eaten like a porridge with meat and vegetables, such as yams or fried cassava.

DIGITAL TRAVELER!
Corn is the fruit of the cereal crop *Zea mays*. Find out why some people call it "corn" and others call it "maize." Where is each name used, and where does "corn" mean any local grain?

5 KĀNGA PIRAU
New Zealand

This tasty Maori porridge is made from fermented corn. It can be eaten with brown sugar and cream or made into a muffin.

Arctic Ocean

EUROPE

ASIA

AFRICA

Pacific Ocean

Indian Ocean

AUSTRALIA

ANTARCTICA

2

3

5

SOUTH AMERICA

A rich BLEND of TASTY DISHES

Extreme features dominate the South American landscape: the towering Andes, the huge Amazon Basin, and the fertile grasslands of the Pampas. The continent is also home to the very dry Atacama Desert, which is one of the most inhospitable environments in the world. Culturally, the continent is quite varied, as well. Indigenous peoples include the Aymara, Quechua, Inca, Yanomami, Mapuche, and Chimú. Their cultures and traditions were greatly changed after the first Spanish and Portuguese explorers and settlers arrived in the 1500s and 1600s. More changes came in time with the arrival of people from Africa, Europe, and Asia, who brought their own cultures and traditions. Today, South American culture and its foods are a creative blend of both indigenous and non-native influences.

This farm, which lies high in the Andes mountains of Peru, grows corn, quinoa, and amaranth.

FOODIE HOT SPOTS

 A SPICY SNACK

In Bolivia, snack on humitas—steamed balls of ground corn mixed with eggs and spices.

 COLORFUL OCAS

These finger-size tubers from Peru are cooked and eaten like potatoes.

 NUTRITIOUS NUTS

In northern Chile, try cookies made with the white insides of small coquito nuts.

 PASTRY PARTY

Celebrate Chile's Independence Day with grape cider and empanadas, or filled pastries.

 FRIED BREAD

Try Guyanese bakes—fried balls of dough that taste great with local peanut butter.

 SURI GRUBS

Eat these skewered, barbecued palm weevil larvae in the markets of Iquitos, Peru.

 CARAMEL COATING

In the Río de la Plata region of Uruguay, spread vanilla-flavored dulce de leche caramel on toast.

 COLD FRESH FISH

Miraflores, Peru, is famous for ceviche—a dish of fish marinated in lime juice.

 CHOCOLATE TREATS

Brazil grows cacao plants and makes brigadeiros—chocolate fudge bites.

FAST FACTS

Size ranking: Fourth largest
Number of countries: 12
Total population: 423,750,000
Largest country by area: Brazil

Caribbean Sea

Caracas

NORTH AMERICA

VENEZUELA

Georgetown

Paramaribo

GUYANA

SURINAME

French Guiana (France)

Bogotá

COLOMBIA

Quito

Galápagos Islands (Ecuador)

ECUADOR

PERU

Lima

BRAZIL

Brasília

Pacific Ocean

BOLIVIA

La Paz

Sucre

PARAGUAY

Asunción

Atlantic Ocean

URUGUAY

CHILE

Santiago

Buenos Aires

Montevideo

ARGENTINA

AUNT BERTHA'S FOOD TRAVEL TIPS

* Be curious! Many South American foods aren't seen in typical Western grocery stores because they haven't been widely distributed to other continents. Keep a list of the new foods you get to taste, and share your experiences with friends and family.

* South (and Central) America is the birthplace of chocolate, but branch out when you order ice cream. Try an unusual fruit flavor such as soursop—it might become a favorite.

* Keep in mind that lunch is the big meal of the day in South America. Most people leave work and enjoy a three-course lunch with their families. Dinner is more of a light snack, like an arepa—a corn cake with a dairy filling or topping—or bread and cheese with a cup of hot chocolate or coffee.

POLITICAL MAP

⊛ National capital

0   600 miles
0   600 kilometers

Falkland Islands (Islas Malvinas) (U.K.)

DELICIOUS CUISINE

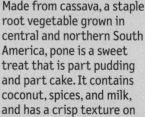

cacao pods growing on a cacao tree in Venezuela

COFFEE, chocolate, cattle, and CORN

Brazil and Argentina are world leaders in food production, with massive farms and ranches, and a big fishing industry. These countries export large amounts of coffee, soybeans, beef, orange juice, and sugar. Corn—a food plant indigenous to the Americas—and wheat are widely grown and are a major part of people's diets throughout the continent. The Pampas grasslands of Argentina, Uruguay, and southern Brazil, and the Llanos tropical grasslands of Colombia and Venezuela are major cattle-raising areas. Sheep are reared in areas where cattle do not thrive, such as Patagonia in Chile and Argentina. Small farms in the Andes raise indigenous animals such as llamas and guinea pigs for food.

Caribbean Sea
3
NORTH AMERICA
Pacific Ocean
COLOMBIA
Galápagos Islands (Ecuador)
ECUADOR
PERU

5 COOL FOODS

1 CASSAVA PONE
Guyana

Made from cassava, a staple root vegetable grown in central and northern South America, pone is a sweet treat that is part pudding and part cake. It contains coconut, spices, and milk, and has a crisp texture on the outside surrounding a gooey middle.

 **APPETIZING ATTRACTIONS**

DIGITAL TRAVELER!
Soursop was one of the first fruits brought from the Americas to other parts of the world. Find out how it is used as a food and where the soursop tree is grown today.

↪ CLOUD FOREST CHOCOLATIERS
Visit El Quetzal, in the small cloud-forest village of Mindo, Ecuador, to see how cacao beans are picked and made into chocolate bars.

↪ FARM EXPERIENCE
At the eco-farm in Matahuasi village, near Huancayo, Peru, learn how local people grow fruits and vegetables and farm sustainably.

↪ DESERT MARKET
At Atacama Farmers Market in San Pedro de Atacama, Chile, enjoy delicious corn dishes during warm days and a cup of hot chocolate to warm you during cold nights.

? DID YOU KNOW?

Chocolate originated in the Americas. However, today's major producers of cacao beans—the raw material for chocolate—are West African countries. Most of the leading manufacturers of chocolate are located in Western Europe, mainly Germany, Switzerland, and Belgium.

2 ACARAJÉ
Brazil

This African-inspired deep-fried patty is a popular street snack in the town of Recife. It's made of smashed black-eyed peas, onions, and a filling of cashew nuts or shrimp. Cashew trees are indigenous to Brazil.

FARMLAND USAGE

Pasture → Cropland

☐ Other land use

3 PAPAS RELLENAS
Colombia

These balls of mashed potato are filled with delicious seasoned beef, then battered and fried. They are usually eaten with rice or salad and fresh salsa. Give these tasty bites a try in the street markets of Cartagena.

VENEZUELA

GUYANA

French Guiana (France)

SURINAME

BRAZIL

BOLIVIA

PARAGUAY

Atlantic Ocean

CHILE

ARGENTINA

URUGUAY

Falkland Islands (Islas Malvinas) (U.K.)

4 QUINDIM
Brazil

Brazil is one of the world's top sugar producers. Sugar from sugarcane is mixed with egg yolks and ground coconut and baked in molds to make quindim, a sweet custard. Quindim is very popular in and around the city of Belém, where coconuts abound.

5 ASADO
Argentina

Argentines love an asado. At this barbecue, family and friends gather to grill all cuts of beef, sausage, lamb, and pork beside a fire and on a grill over burning coals and wood. They also cook and serve chicken and vegetables.

33

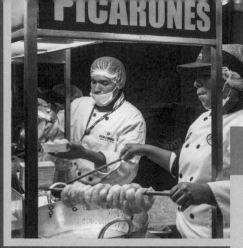

1 PICARONES
Peru

Street vendors in the cities of Miraflores and Lima, Peru's capital, make and sell these treats. The cinnamon-and-sugar-covered doughnuts are often made from the flour of indigenous sweet potatoes. Watch as the rings of dough are tossed into a vat of hot oil and then plucked out to eat.

2 LLAPINGACHOS
Ecuador

These tasty fried potato, onion, and cheese pancakes from the city of Ambato are served with a creamy peanut sauce. Often, they are served alongside avocado, a fried egg, or a cured smoked sausage.

? DID YOU KNOW?

Tubers are swollen underground parts of some plants that store nutrients for the following year's growth. Potato and oca tubers are stemlike, with "eyes" that can grow shoots; cassavas and others are rootlike.

3 PEPPERPOT
Guyana

Get in the holiday spirit with this national dish of Guyana made with meat, cinnamon, chili pepper, and cassareep, a thick dark sauce made from the cassava root. Pepperpot is often served at Christmas and weddings.

Caribbean Sea

NORTH AMERICA

VENEZUELA

French Guiana (France)

SURINAME

GUYANA

Atlantic Ocean

COLOMBIA

Galápagos Islands (Ecuador)

ECUADOR

PERU

BRAZIL

BOLIVIA

Pacific Ocean

PARAGUAY

CHILE

ROOTS and TUBERS PRODUCTION*
U.S. tons per acre (metric tons per hectare)

- ■ More than 5.7 (12.7)
- ■ 5.7 (12.7) or less
- □ 0

*Not all roots and tubers shown

URUGUAY

ARGENTINA

DIGITAL TRAVELER!
French fries, chips, or potato fritters—find out how and where the popular deep-fried slices of potato get their names and how they are eaten.

Falkland Islands (Islas Malvinas) (U.K.)

cassavas and sweet potatoes

TASTY TUBERS

POTATOES, cassavas, and root VEGGIES

The high altitude and extreme conditions of the Andes are not suitable for growing most foods, but this harsh environment is a perfect place for root and tuber crops to thrive. In fact, this is where people first cultivated potatoes. From potatoes to oca, from mashua to ulluco, roots and tubers from this region find their way onto plates and into sweet treats all over South America. In addition, the Amazon rainforest provides an assortment of leaves and spices that flavor our foods.

4 CHIMICHURRI
Argentina

This flavorful sauce is made from chopped parsley leaves and garlic bulbs, oil, chili pepper, and vinegar. In Buenos Aires, you'll find it served with steaks. Taste the sauce first before pouring it onto your meal. It can be quite spicy!

5 PAPAS A LA HUANCAINA
Bolivia

Originating from Huancayo, Peru, this dish of sliced boiled potatoes, hard-boiled eggs, lettuce, and olives can be covered with a cheese sauce and eaten cold as an appetizer. In Bolivia, people add a peanut sauce, and the dish is usually served as a main course while the sauce is still warm.

APPETIZING ATTRACTIONS

↘ SAMPLE NEW FOODS
Mercado del Puerto, an indoor and outdoor market in Montevideo, Uruguay, is a great spot for sampling french fries with spicy sauces.

↘ EXPLORE THE JUNGLE
At Museu da Amazônia in Manaus, Brazil, you can enjoy a jungle walk, see all kinds of food plants and Amazonian fish, and learn about the planting, harvesting, and making of manioc, a staple food that is also known as cassava.

↘ CHILL OUT WITH PLANTS
Spend a day at the Botanical Gardens in Bogotá, Colombia, to learn how scientists study the ways food plants react to climate change and naturally combat diseases and pollution.

CHOICE FOODS

cocona (top left), pomegranate (back), papaya (right), and cherimoya (front)

CRUNCHY, fleshy, stringy, and SWEET

The Amazon rainforest and mountains of South America are filled with fruits of all shapes, sizes, and flavors. Some, including avocados and bananas, are likely familiar. Others, such as soursop and Amazonian pear, might not be. With such a range, there's plenty to try. Trees in this region produce a bounty of nuts, including cashews, cacao, coquito, and Brazil nuts. There are lots of legumes, too. String beans, kidney beans, and butter beans, used in all kinds of dishes, are all indigenous to South America.

APPETIZING ATTRACTIONS

COLORFUL MARKET
The Ecuadorian city of Otavalo, which is surrounded by towering volcanoes, is well known for its huge historic market. There you will find fruits and beans of all colors, shapes, and sizes—as well as guinea pigs, which are a popular local food.

COFFEE TRADING ROOM
The Museu do Café is an opulent building in Santos, Brazil, with a stained-glass ceiling. Once a busy place where traders bought and sold Brazilian coffee, it now has displays that show everything from how to use coffee grounds in desserts to how they can help flavor meat dishes.

LOCAL FOOD SHOPPING
In Santiago, Chile, explore a tostaduria—a large store that sells all kinds of local spices, grains, fruits, and nuts. You can pick and choose the foods you want to try from an array of open displays.

5 COOL FOODS

1 TOSTONES
Venezuela

Try these twice-fried, flattened plantain slices as a snack or with your lunch. Plantains are a type of banana but are not usually eaten raw. In Venezuela they are fried and often served as a side dish. You can top them with sour cream, cheese, salsa, or beans.

2 ACAI
Brazil

Pronounced *a-sah-EE*, these purple berries are the fruits of a palm tree indigenous to the Amazon region of Brazil. The berries are often pulped and served as a frozen sorbet dessert with granola, strawberries, and banana. Acai juices and smoothies are also popular.

! STRANGE BUT TRUE
Lucuma is a South American fruit commonly known as eggfruit. Its ripe flesh has a flavor similar to that of a roasted sweet potato, but the texture is like that of a hard-boiled egg yolk. The flesh is often pureed and used to make ice cream.

3 LOCRO
Argentina

This tasty stew of lima beans, corn, squash, and meat is always served on May 25, Independence Day in Argentina. But it is widely available throughout the year. On Independence Day, buy locro at a street stall in Córdoba and enjoy your meal while watching fireworks.

DIGITAL TRAVELER!
South American beans include runner, string, snap, and winged. Grab an adult and go online to find out how they are grown, harvested, and sold.

FRUIT PRODUCTION*
U.S. tons per acre
(metric tons per hectare)
- More than 10.7 (24)
- 10.7 (24) or less
- 0

*Not all fruits shown

Caribbean Sea

NORTH AMERICA

VENEZUELA

GUYANA

French Guiana (France)

SURINAME

COLOMBIA

ECUADOR

Galápagos Islands (Ecuador)

PERU

Pacific Ocean

BRAZIL

BOLIVIA

Atlantic Ocean

PARAGUAY

CHILE

ARGENTINA

URUGUAY

Falkland Islands (Islas Malvinas) (U.K.)

4 GULUPA
Colombia

Related to passion fruit and often called sugar apple or sweetsop, gulupa comes from Colombia. It looks like a small purple golf ball, but the inside flesh is soft and sweet and can be spooned on yogurt, made into a juice, or eaten by itself. It has a strong smell and a unique flavor.

5 CHERIMOYA
Peru

Author Mark Twain called this South American fruit "the most delicious fruit known to men." Indigenous to Peru, it smells like pineapple or pear. At street stalls in Lima, you'll see locals cut the fruit open, scoop out the flesh with their fingers, and eat it. In English, this fruit is called a custard apple.

FESTIVALS AND FEASTS

CELEBRATING WITH FOOD

Carnival parade, Rio de Janeiro, Brazil

A FIESTA of FLAVOR

It's time for a fiesta! South Americans have been celebrating Earth and its bounty of foods for millennia. *Fiestas*, the Spanish word for "festivals," are celebrated throughout this continent. Foods from the rainforest, fresh fish from the waters, and regional delights from cities and villages are enjoyed by all. Carnival—the food and parade festival held immediately before the long pre-Easter fast of Lent—is also widely celebrated. These events, which are open to visitors, provide many opportunities to experience the unique and colorful foods of the area.

5 COOL FOOD EVENTS

1 Argentina
2 Chile
3 Ecuador
4 Brazil
5 Peru

1 FISHERS' FESTIVAL
Argentina

At this festival held during the second half of January in the seaside city of Mar del Plata, you'll get a chance to taste traditional fish and shellfish dishes made by local fishers. Some local restaurants also cook large paellas—a rice and seafood dish—for people to share.

2 ÑAM FESTIVAL
Chile

Each spring in Santiago, you can enjoy and take part in four days of food-related family activities featuring meals made from local ingredients. No matter what you like to eat or drink, you're likely to find something to suit your taste buds.

TRY THIS RECIPE

CHIMICHURRI SAUCE

A TASTE OF ARGENTINA

This tasty sauce is traditionally used as a condiment or marinade on grilled meats. But it can also be mixed with vegetables or rice, sprinkled on eggs, used as salad dressing, or even enjoyed as a tortilla chip dip.

Prep time: 10 minutes
Serves: 4 people

1 cup fresh parsley leaves
3 to 4 garlic cloves
¼ small red onion
2 tablespoons fresh oregano leaves
½ cup extra virgin olive oil
2 tablespoons red wine vinegar
½ teaspoon sea salt
⅛ teaspoon black pepper
¼ teaspoon red pepper flakes

1. Have an adult finely chop the parsley, garlic, onion, and oregano.
2. Place the finely chopped parsley, garlic, onion, and oregano in a small bowl.
3. Stir in the olive oil, vinegar, salt, pepper, and red pepper flakes.
4. Let the mixture sit for at least an hour or two before using.

SOUTH AMERICA

3 INTI RAYMI
Ecuador

This ancient celebration, held June 21–24, celebrates the Inca new year and honors the Inca sun god, Inti, for allowing crops to grow. It originated in Cusco, Peru, but is now celebrated throughout the Andes highlands by the indigenous Quechua people, descendants of the ancient Inca. In Otavalo, Ecuador, people celebrate Inti Raymi with a week of celebration that includes eating lots of fruit and corn-based dishes.

DIGITAL TRAVELER!

In Cardal, Uruguay, locals hold a milk festival each October. They create a giant dessert for people to share. Find out what the dessert is and how many people it can feed.

4 BRASIL SABOR
Brazil

Sabor is the Portuguese word for "flavor." Portuguese is the most commonly spoken language in Brazil. Each May at the Festival Brasil Sabor, restaurants throughout the country serve special dishes that represent their own local food traditions. It is a great time to travel to Brazil and experience the diversity of local foods.

5 MISTURA FOOD FESTIVAL
Peru

Join up to 400,000 people in Lima in September for the largest food festival in South America. Peruvian cooks not only make and serve local foods, but also try their hand at making dishes from around the world.

KERNEL CREATIONS

FLATBREADS, stews, and CORN DRINKS

an Aymara woman in Peru grinding wheat to make flour

The kernels, or seeds, of grain crops are ground and milled into flours, roasted whole, and cooked into a variety of foods. South Americans enjoy a rich array of kernels, but corn takes center stage. Peru alone has about 55 varieties of corn that are used to make a range of different foods. But corn isn't the only grain popular in South America. This continent is also the origin of two important non-cereal grains, quinoa and amaranth. These protein-rich grains are grown in the Andes mountains.

APPETIZING ATTRACTIONS

➥ TRY AMAZON LIVING
Venture into the Brazilian Amazon for a stay at an eco-lodge. Experience the rich Amazon culture and sample local foods such as pão de queijo—baked cheese and bread balls.

➥ MAKE YOUR OWN CHOCOLATE
Journey to Ollantaytambo, a village in Peru's Sacred Valley, to visit a chocolate museum. There you can learn how chocolate is made and create and eat your own chocolate treats.

➥ BE AN AGROTOURIST
In the Patagonia region of Argentina, stay at an approved agrotourist site to experience village and farm life and try local foods. You can spend time with local families to discover their culture and special food traditions.

5 COOL FOODS

1 AREPAS
Venezuela

These tasty corn flatbreads or pockets can be found throughout the country served with cheese, avocado, or egg toppings or fillings. They make a great start to the day or a snack at any time.

2 CHOCLO CON QUESO
Ecuador

Choclo is an Andean corn with large kernels that is often cooked and served on the cob with queso fresco, or fresh cheese. You can find choclo con queso at street vendors in every town. It is eaten on its own or as a side for meat dishes.

Caribbean Sea

NORTH AMERICA

Pacific Ocean

VENEZUELA ❶

GUYANA

French Guiana (France)

SURINAME

Galápagos Islands (Ecuador)

COLOMBIA

ECUADOR ❷

PERU ❸

BRAZIL

BOLIVIA ❹

Atlantic Ocean

PARAGUAY ❺

CHILE

ARGENTINA

URUGUAY

Falkland Islands (Islas Malvinas) (U.K.)

DIGITAL TRAVELER!
Find out why cereal and non-cereal grains don't grow well in Patagonia but thrive elsewhere in the Andes mountains.

GRAIN PRODUCTION*
U.S. tons per acre (metric tons per hectare)
- More than 0.1 (0.3)
- 0.1 (0.3) or less
- 0
*Not all grains shown

3 CHICHA MORADA
Peru

This refreshing juice is made from boiled purple corn mixed with a bit of cinnamon, clove, and sometimes pineapple and strawberry. You can get this popular drink at food stalls and cafés in Lima, as well as many other places throughout the country.

4 QUINOA
Bolivia

This grain comes from the Altiplano plateau area of the Andes. Quinoa has been cultivated for centuries in Bolivia. The quinoa plant produces grains, but it is not a cereal or member of the grass family. It is part of the spinach family. Protein-rich quinoa comes in many colors. Locals use it in everything from stews and soups to vegetable pies.

STRANGE BUT TRUE

Andean kiwicha, also known as Peruvian amaranth, is a non-cereal plant that produces grains that have almost all the nutrients people need to stay healthy. The grains are rich in protein, minerals, and several vitamins.

5 SOPA PARAGUAYA
Paraguay

Although *sopa* means "soup," this national dish is actually a dense cornbread made with cheese, milk, and eggs that you will often find in Paraguay's capital, Asunción. It is popular at weddings and parties.

5 COOL FOODS

DIGITAL TRAVELER!
Find out which South American country is the continent's largest producer and exporter of beef. Which countries buy most of its beef?

1 SALCHIPAPAS
Ecuador

These fried hot dogs are served with french fries and ketchup or mayonnaise. In street markets, they're sold as a finger food. In restaurants, they are served as an appetizer.

2 SALTEÑAS
Bolivia

Many varieties of little stuffed pastries filled with meat stew can be found all over South America, but these boatlike salteñas are particularly popular in Bolivia. Eat these snacks warm with a dipping sauce.

3 COXINHAS
Brazil

These deep-fried breaded balls of creamy shredded chicken can be found in market stalls all over Brazil. In some regions, coxinhas are filled with cheese. They are almost as popular as soccer and Carnival! They are often eaten as a snack.

Caribbean Sea

NORTH AMERICA

VENEZUELA

GUYANA

SURINAME

COLOMBIA

French Guiana (France)

Galápagos Islands (Ecuador)

ECUADOR

Atlantic Ocean

PERU

BRAZIL

Pacific Ocean

BOLIVIA

PARAGUAY

CHILE

ARGENTINA

URUGUAY

Falkland Islands (Islas Malvinas) (U.K.)

CATTLE PRODUCTION
Number per square mile
(number per square kilometer)

■ More than 129 (50)
■ 129 (50) or less
□ 0

42

LIVESTOCK AND MORE

DELICIOUS DISHES

eggs for sale at a warehouse in Bogotá, Colombia

GRILLED, fried, or BARBECUED

While most of the foods of South America's mountain regions are grain- and bean-based, and those in the Amazon region are fish-based, meat is big on the plains. Ranches on the Pampas supply beef for locals and tourists. Argentines, in particular, enjoy barbecues and mixed grills. In Patagonia, sheep farming is widespread. The national delicacy of Peru is the indigenous cuy, or guinea pig, which is often served roasted. Many people living outside the cities raise their own chickens. People raise llamas and alpacas on farms, especially in the Andes, partly for meat or to carry heavy loads but mostly for hair fiber to make clothing.

APPETIZING ATTRACTIONS

↳ DISCOVER GAUCHO CULTURE
Visit the Gaucho Museum in Montevideo, Uruguay, to see displays and exhibits of equipment used by these South American cowboys on the cattle ranches of the Pampas plains.

↳ A MARKETPLACE MEDLEY
Paloquemao Market in Bogotá, Colombia, is full of stalls selling all kinds of meats, eggs, fish, and dairy products. Try a breakfast snack of empanadas filled with beef.

↳ DINE IN A BARN
For mouthwatering meat dishes and a unique dining experience, savor the foods at Xapuri Restaurante in the city of Belo Horizonte in Brazil. This restaurant is set inside a barn with a thatched roof and wooden tables.

4 CHORIZO
Argentina

You can find this tasty, spicy sausage on most menus in Argentina. It is made from highly seasoned chopped or ground pork that is smoked and sometimes cut into slices. Eat it with eggs for breakfast, with salad for an appetizer, or as part of a paella, a traditional rice dish.

5 CHURRASCO
Chile

Churrasco is the name for any thin slice of meat—usually beef—that is grilled over hot coals or fried in a very hot skillet. It is served throughout South America, but is particularly popular in Chile, Brazil, and Argentina. Churrasco is served with chimichurri sauce.

! STRANGE BUT TRUE
Guinea pigs—cuyes to Andean people—are not pigs and they're not from the African country Guinea. They are rodents, in the same South American family of animals as capybaras, cavies, and maras. They were domesticated more than 3,000 years ago in the Andes and have been an important part of South American cultures and diets ever since.

MILK MAGIC

CHEESE and MORE

The dairy industry of South America is small but growing fast. Family-run businesses, not large companies, produce most of the continent's milk, cheese, and yogurts. The people of Brazil consume lots of cow's milk.

Cheeses are very popular in Argentina, Chile, and Colombia, and yogurt is eaten all over South America. Dairy is also becoming more popular as a breakfast food, and dairy products are used widely in cooking.

Argentine cheese for sale

5 COOL FOODS

1 DULCE DE LECHE
Argentina

This sticky, sweet brown mix of milk and caramelized sugar ends up in all sorts of recipes in Argentina. In the city of Córdoba, it is used in and on pastries and cookies, as a sauce over ice cream, on waffles, and as the filling in birthday cakes.

2 PÃO DE QUEIJO
Brazil

Pão de queijo is Portuguese for "cheese bread." These small gluten-free rolls are made with tapioca flour mixed with eggs and cheese made from cow's milk originating in the Brazilian state of Minas Gerais. They are baked and usually eaten warm for breakfast or as a snack at any time of day.

APPETIZING ATTRACTIONS

▶ A FROZEN FAVORITE

The city of Ibarra, Ecuador, is the birthplace of *helado de paila*—meaning "ice cream from a pail." It is a mix of ice, sugar, and local fruits that become frozen as they are mixed in a large bronze bowl over a block of ice and salt. It is an ice cream for the lactose-intolerant. Choose your flavor and enjoy!

▶ DESSERT IN A DESERT

In the desert town of San Pedro de Atacama, Chile, try the local fruit pepino dulce, or melon pear. Top it with ice cream flavored with rica rica, an herb from an indigenous wild shrub. Together they will give you a mixture of lovely tastes.

▶ RATE THE RECIPES

Travel to northeastern Brazil and try different recipes for canjica, a mixture of white corn, coconut milk, and condensed cow's milk made into a porridge-like dessert. People in each town or village have their own twist. Some sprinkle cinnamon or cloves on top, while others add peanuts, or grated coconut.

RECORD BREAKER

Locro de papa is an Ecuadorian potato and cheese soup. The single largest batch of the soup ever made was created at a charity event in 2017 in the capital city of Quito. It weighed 12,760 pounds (5,788 kg).

MILK PRODUCTION

U.S. tons per acre
(metric tons per hectare)

- More than 0.1 (0.2)
- 0.02–0.1 (0.05–0.2)
- 0.01–0.02 (0.03–0.05)
- 0.004–0.009 (0.01–0.02)
- Less than 0.004 (0.01)
- No data

Caribbean Sea

NORTH AMERICA

Pacific Ocean

Atlantic Ocean

VENEZUELA

GUYANA

SURINAME

French Guiana (France)

COLOMBIA

ECUADOR

Galápagos Islands (Ecuador)

PERU

BRAZIL

BOLIVIA

PARAGUAY

CHILE

ARGENTINA

URUGUAY

Falkland Islands (Islas Malvinas) (U.K.)

5 CHOCOLATE SANTAFEREÑO
Colombia

Try this hot chocolate drink in one of Bogotá's oldest restaurants, La Puerta Falsa. You'll find a surprise at the bottom of your cup—salty white cheese called queso campesino.

DIGITAL TRAVELER!

Did you know you can drink the milk of llamas and alpacas? Find out how the protein, fat, and minerals of their milk compare to those in cow's milk.

3 EMBORRAJADOS
Ecuador

This Ecuadorian snack is made from thick slices of fresh cheese sandwiched between ripened, flattened plantains. The whole thing is dipped in a batter of wheat flour and egg and then deep fried. The sandwich is eaten nice and hot.

4 DULCE DE GUAYABA
Paraguay

Guayaba is the Spanish word for the guava fruit. Try this popular dessert, which consists of slices of boiled guava paste served with thick pieces of semihard white cheese.

45

COASTAL RICHES

catching tarpon and corvina off the coast of Venezuela

COD, crayfish, and BARNACLES

The nutrient-rich waters off South America's Pacific and Atlantic coasts are home to huge populations of fish and shellfish. Both small- and large-scale fishing fleets harvest from these waters. Anchovies are caught in great quantities off the coasts of Peru and Chile. Ecuador's waters are rich in shrimp. The Amazon Basin's lakes and rivers are home to all kinds of freshwater fish. But overfishing is causing problems for fish and other seafood populations. To help protect species, aquaculture—the farming of fish, shellfish, seaweed, and other marine and freshwater species—is now being used all over South America.

APPETIZING ATTRACTIONS

➥ STEW ON THE COAST
The red cusk-eel is a marine fish of the South Pacific Ocean. In the city of Arica, in northern Chile, try caldillo de congrio, a delicious seafood stew made with red cusk-eel (congrio), tomatoes, and potatoes.

➥ FISHY FRENCH CONNECTION
The Mercado Adolpho Lisboa in Manaus, Brazil, is a marketplace resembling the old Les Halles market in Paris, France. Fish from the Amazon River, such as the tambaqui and pirarucu, are sold here.

➥ POP-UP PICANTERÍAS
In Arequipa, Peru, these family-run lunchtime restaurants serve fish dishes like locally caught sea trout that is grilled or fried and served with potatoes.

5 COOL FOODS

1 ENCEBOLLADO
Ecuador

This popular seafood soup is made of tuna, red onions, cassava, and tomato. Try it at any coastal resort, along with plantain chips and bread. Use the bread to soak up the mouthwatering liquid.

2 CORVINA
Guyana

If you like your cooked fish light and flaky, corvina is for you. Corvina is a marine fish found at local fish markets along the coasts. In Guyana, try it baked, grilled, or fried served with butter, garlic, and a side of vegetables.

4 PICOROCO
Chile

These giant barnacles can be found along the rocky shores of Chile. Their cooked meat tastes very much like crab. Add a squeeze of lemon and eat these barnacles straight from the shell. Or enjoy the meat as part of a local seafood soup.

SOUTH AMERICA

3 CHUPE DE CAMARONES
Peru

Arequipa is the home of this tasty chowder, traditionally made with crayfish or shrimp. It combines chunky vegetables such as onions, peas, and peppers with milk, poached eggs, and spices.

DIGITAL TRAVELER!
Piranhas are South American fish with a flesh-eating reputation. Find out about tambaqui fish, which are sold at food markets as "vegetarian piranhas."

5 BACALHAU
Brazil

Flattened salted cod is sold at grocery stores all over Brazil. It's used to make fish cake appetizers or as a snack with mashed potatoes and cheese gratin. It's also an ingredient in bacalhau à Gomes de Sá, a traditional dish of fish, eggs, and olives between layers of potato.

Caribbean Sea

NORTH AMERICA

VENEZUELA

French Guiana (France)

SURINAME

GUYANA

COLOMBIA

Galápagos Islands (Ecuador)

ECUADOR

PERU

BRAZIL

Pacific Ocean

BOLIVIA

PARAGUAY

CHILE

AMOUNT OF FISH CAUGHT
Average pounds (kilograms) per person per year

■	More than 132 (60)
■	68–132 (31–60)
■	46–67 (21–30)
■	11–45 (5–20)
□	Less than 11 (5)

URUGUAY

ARGENTINA

STRANGE BUT TRUE

Today, Chileans make stews, salads, and other meals using bull kelp, an edible seaweed found just off the country's coast. Evidence of this seaweed being used as food has been found in an ancient 14,000-year-old hearth excavated in southern Chile.

Falkland Islands (Islas Malvinas) (U.K.)

CRAZY FOR CHOCOLATE

a selection of chocolates

SWEET treats from CACAO beans

This delectable treat, made from the beans of cacao plants of South and Central America, wasn't always so sweet. Long ago, the ancient Olmec made cacao beans into a bitter fermented beverage. Later, the Maya and Aztec roasted and ground the beans and then mixed the paste with water, vanilla, honey, chili, and other spices to create a tasty frothy drink. Over the years, cacao beans have been traded, used as money, and eaten by royalty. Spanish settlers were the first to introduce cacao beans to Spain and the rest of Europe. In Europe the beans were roasted to high temperatures, ground, and mixed with sugar and water or milk to make the chocolate we know. Today, chocolate is eaten in many forms and in many dishes, all over the world.

TRUE OR FALSE?

Which of these statements about chocolate are true and which are false?

1. Buying chocolate labeled "fair trade" helps farmers and workers.
2. Eating large amounts of chocolate can be toxic to dogs.
3. Chocolate melts at a human's body temperature.
4. Chocolate was first created about 500 years ago.
5. It takes 400 to 500 cacao beans to make one pound (.45 kg) of chocolate.

5 COOL FOODS

1 CHOCOLATE SOUFFLÉ
France

Invented in 1783 in the Grande Taverne de Londres, a restaurant in Paris, the chocolate soufflé is one of the fanciest chocolate desserts in the world and takes the most time to create—up to an hour and a half. *Soufflé* is the French word for "breath," so this egg, flour, and chocolate treat is meant to be light and airy.

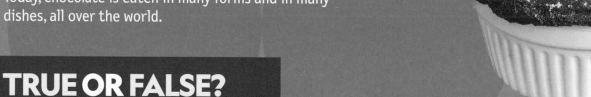

2 CHOCOLATE MOCHI
Japan

These balls of sticky rice dough have a sweet, creamy filling. Sometimes they're filled with ice cream (the rice dough covering keeps the filling from melting in your hands!). Flavors to choose from include chocolate and a sweet red bean paste. Eat them as a snack or for dessert.

See answers on page 150.

3 AFGHAN COOKIES
New Zealand

Nobody really knows how these small, round chocolate cookies got their name, but they're a classic in New Zealand. Made out of butter, sugar, flour, cocoa powder, and unsweetened cornflakes, they're topped with a chocolate icing and pieces of walnut. These sweet treats are traditionally eaten as an afternoon snack.

4 CHAMPURRADO
Mexico

In Mexico it's easy to find a chocolate drink that suits your taste. Champurrado may be one of them. It is a hot drink made with corn flour and milk and flavored with spices and chocolate. It's often served for breakfast to warm you up after a cool night.

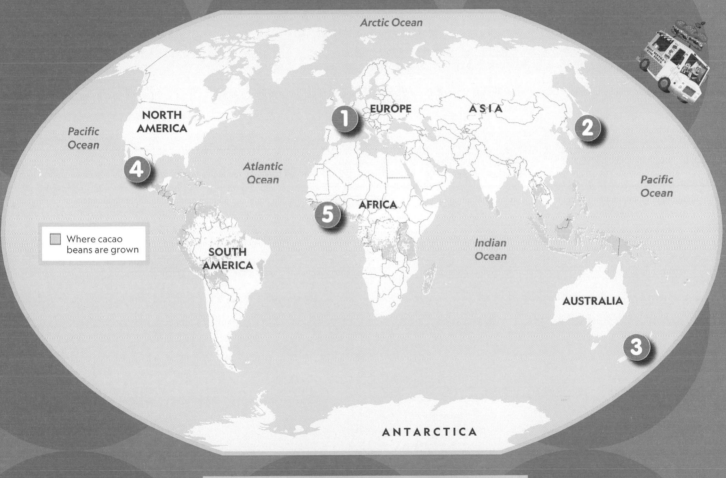

Arctic Ocean

NORTH AMERICA

Pacific Ocean

Atlantic Ocean

EUROPE

ASIA

1

2

Pacific Ocean

AFRICA

5

Where cacao beans are grown

SOUTH AMERICA

Indian Ocean

AUSTRALIA

3

ANTARCTICA

5 CHOCOLATE BLENDS
Côte d'Ivoire

This African country is the world's leading producer of cacao beans. It grows many varieties and makes both semisweet and bittersweet chocolate. Find your favorite!

DIGITAL TRAVELER!
Chocolate bars such as Milky Way and Twix are sold around the world under different names. Find another name for the Snickers bar and when and where it was sold.

49

EUROPE

FANTASTIC foods of many FLAVORS

From freezing Iceland in the North Atlantic Ocean to sunny Greece in the Mediterranean Sea, from the low plains of the Netherlands to the mighty Alps and Caucasus peaks, Europe spans a variety of climates—and cuisines. About 40 percent of Europe's land is covered with farmland and pastures. A lot of food in Europe also comes from the surrounding seas. Traditional diets in different countries are as varied as the landscapes, depending on locally available ingredients and the influences of other cultures—conquerors or colonies—throughout history.

Small farms with grazing land dot the hills and mountain slopes of Switzerland.

FOODIE HOT SPOTS

 GROWING GRAINS

See crops grow in Ukraine's rich soils, including winter wheat used to make bread.

 FLUFFY POTATOES

Belarusians say their native potatoes make their draniki—potato pancakes—really fluffy.

 OLIVE GROVES

In Greece, see groves of trees bearing olives, which are fresh-picked and then cured.

 ARTICHOKE ART

At a festival in Ladispoli, Italy, see sculptors make art out of artichokes.

 CRISPY WAFFLES

Eat two crispy waffles with a layer of caramel in between—that's a Dutch stroopwafel!

 GREAT GOULASH

Hungary is famous for goulash, a red-colored beef stew seasoned with Hungarian paprika.

 DELICIOUS DIP

Try Swiss fondue, and use a long fork to dip pieces of bread into a pot of melted cheese.

 FINE FISH

Norwegian herring is smoked, salted, or pickled. In places, it's a popular finger food.

 CREATIVE CHEESES

Europe makes delicious cheeses that are enjoyed by people all over the world.

FAST FACTS

Size ranking: Sixth largest
Number of countries: 46 (including Russia)
Total population: 751,632,000
Largest country entirely in Europe by area: Ukraine

Barents Sea

ICELAND
Reykjavík

Norwegian Sea

SWEDEN

FINLAND

NORWAY
Oslo
Helsinki
Stockholm
Tallinn
ESTONIA

RUSSIA

A commonly accepted division between Asia and Europe is formed by the Ural Mountains, Ural River, Caspian Sea, Caucasus Mountains, and the Black Sea with its outlets to the Aegean Sea, the Bosporus, and the Dardanelles. A small part of Turkey is in Europe.

UNITED KINGDOM
Scotland

North Sea

Riga
LATVIA

Moscow

N. Ireland

DENMARK

LITHUANIA
Vilnius
Minsk

IRELAND (ÉIRE)
Dublin

Copenhagen

Kaliningrad (Russia)

BELARUS

KAZAKHSTAN

Wales
England
London
NETH.
The Hague
Amsterdam
Berlin
Warsaw
Kyev

POLAND

Brussels
BELGIUM
GERMANY

UKRAINE

Atlantic Ocean

Paris
LUXEMBOURG
Prague
CZECHIA (CZECH REP.)
SLOVAKIA

Bratislava
Vienna

MOLDOVA
Chișinău

LIECHTENSTEIN
SWITZ.
Bern
AUSTRIA
Budapest
HUNGARY

CRIMEA

FRANCE

Bay of Biscay

SLOVENIA
Ljubljana
Zagreb
CROATIA

ROMANIA

Caspian Sea

Sarajevo
BOSNIA & HERZEGOVINA
Belgrade
SERBIA
Bucharest

Black Sea

GEORGIA

AZERBAIJAN
Baku

PORTUGAL
ANDORRA
MONACO
SAN MARINO
ITALY
MONTENEGRO
Podgorica

KOSOVO
Pristina
BULGARIA
Sofia

Lisbon
Madrid
SPAIN
VATICAN CITY
Rome
Skopje
NORTH MACEDONIA

TURKEY

ASIA

Gibraltar (U.K.)
Tirana
ALBANIA

Mediterranean Sea

GREECE

POLITICAL MAP
⊛ National capital
▢ Small country

AFRICA
Valletta
MALTA
Athens

Nicosia
CYPRUS

0   400 miles
0   400 kilometers

AUNT BERTHA'S FOOD TRAVEL TIPS

* Look for farmers markets and produce stands where you can find fresh local products. Many stalls offer seasonal samples you can try.

* Although tap water is safe to drink in many European countries, you should always check to see if it is safer to drink bottled water in a place you are visiting.

* Plan a picnic! Europe has lots of nice parks, and plenty of shops that sell bread, cheese, fruit, yogurt, and treats—everything you need for a pleasant open-air lunch.

WORKING THE LAND

people harvesting olives in Portugal

From APPLE ORCHARDS to OLIVE GROVES

Farmers around the Mediterranean Sea were among the first people to grow wheat and barley and raise sheep, goats, and cows. Most of Europe's farms and orchards are family-run, raising a variety of crops and livestock. There are multigenerational families carrying on traditions, young people introducing new products and organic farming methods, and some large farms using the latest technology. The olive groves of southern Europe are hundreds of years old. Among Europe's top agricultural products are wheat, milk, beets, corn, and potatoes. Pork, beef, chicken, apples, and a range of fresh vegetables are also popular.

APPETIZING ATTRACTIONS

SUNFLOWER FIELDS
In the Italian regions of Tuscany, Umbria, and Marche, farmers plant rows of bright sunflowers to harvest the seeds for sunflower oil. The waving fields of colorful blooms are a lovely summer sight.

DEHESAS AND PIGS
You might recognize Spain's dehesas from the children's book *The Story of Ferdinand*. Dehesas are ecosystems of oak forests and grasses, where Iberian pigs—the source of Spain's ibérico ham—and fighting bulls are raised. Ibérico ham has a distinct flavor related to the pigs' diet of acorns.

TRADITIONAL FARMS
Romania's Piatra Craiului National Park preserves not only wildlife, but also small traditional farms along the steep hillsides. You might spot sheep grazing in orchards, farmers driving horse-drawn carts, or families selling local farm foods.

5 COOL FOODS

1 BEET BISCUITS
Poland

Many Polish farms grow sugar beets—the swollen root of the *Beta vulgaris* plant—and use the sugar for foods like biscuits. The first factory ever to extract sugar from these beets was built here in 1802. About one-third of the world's sugar comes from sugar beets. The rest comes from sugarcane stems.

2 TOMATES FARCIES
France

For a classic Mediterranean dish, try these French stuffed tomatoes. Large, ripe tomatoes are hollowed out, then stuffed with onions, garlic, herbs, olive oil, rice, and perhaps cheese and ground beef. The filled tomatoes are baked for about an hour and eaten warm.

3 FRIED POTATOES
Belgium

In Belgium, frites—also known as french fries or chips—are a popular food. Street vendors serve frites in cardboard or paper cones with a choice of mayonnaise-based sauces.

DIGITAL TRAVELER!
With an adult's help, use a travel guide or geography app, or search online to discover the best time to try locally grown foods in the places you want to visit.

FARMLAND USAGE

Pasture　　Cropland

☐ Other land use

EUROPE

4 CHARD
Switzerland

The leafy green vegetable also known as Swiss chard is not native to Switzerland, though it grows there. Chard originated in southern Europe and is now grown widely throughout the continent. It's easy to grow, nutritious, and a bright addition to salads.

5 FRIED BREAD
Lithuania

Rye is a grain grown in many Eastern European countries. In Lithuania, kepta duona, or fried bread, is a popular snack. It's dark rye bread fried in oil and seasoned with garlic and salt.

? DID YOU KNOW?

Some European farmers grow crops to produce electricity. In Italy's Po Valley, farmers put corn, other crops, and waste products into a digester to make bio-gas. The bio-gas is burned to make electricity.

NATURE'S BOUNTY

From TURNIPS to KALE

R oot vegetables such as carrots, turnips, and beets are valuable food sources because they're nutritious and long-lasting. Usually harvested in the fall, they can survive storage over a long winter. A potato is also a root, but it's a tuber—a single potato plant will form many potatoes underground. Potato plants are adaptable and don't require very fertile soils. They grow in much of central and northern Europe, even high up in the Alps. Leafy vegetables, such as spinach and kale, grow especially well in southern Europe. The winters are warm there, which means a perfect climate for these crops to grow.

European root and leaf crops

DIGITAL TRAVELER!

Grab an adult and go online to look up a Harry Potter potion using scurvy grass. Then find photos of the plant, which grows naturally along many coastal areas of Europe. Long ago, it was an important food source for sailors, who relied on it to fend off scurvy—a disease caused by lack of vitamin C.

WHITE ASPARAGUS

Europeans get excited when white asparagus is harvested each spring. You won't see green sprouts in the fields because this crop grows underground. Look for springtime white asparagus piled up at the Bastille Market in Paris.

HISTORICAL FARM

At Acton Scott Farm in Shropshire, England, you can see a 19th-century farmhouse, old farm equipment, and horses pulling plows, or take a walk on footpaths through the fields, buy some tasty produce, and grab a home-cooked meal at the café.

BIO BRASS

To learn about organic vegetable farming, stop by the Bio Brass visitor center in Zeewolde, Netherlands. The Bio Brass company produces celery, cauliflower, broccoli, cabbage, lettuce, parsnips, and more.

5 COOL FOODS

1 BRUSSELS SPROUTS
United Kingdom

These tiny cabbage look-alikes, native to the Mediterranean region, are a traditional Sunday roast dish in England. Popular recipes add bacon and chestnuts fried in bacon fat, with butter for good measure.

2 LANTTULAATIKKO
Finland

Rutabagas, or *lanttu* in Finnish, also called Swedish turnips, are believed to be a cross between a turnip and a wild cabbage. Finns make them into a casserole called lanttulaatikko, using rutabagas baked with cream, ginger, nutmeg, cinnamon, and egg. It is a traditional dish popular at Christmastime. The roots can also be eaten raw, pickled, or boiled and mashed.

RECORD BREAKER

How fast could you consume 2.5 cups (85 g) of leafy green watercress and a small bottle of water? Every May, watercress eaters compete at the Alresford Watercress Festival in Hampshire, England, U.K. The record time is less than a minute!

ROOTS and TUBERS PRODUCTION*
U.S. tons per acre (metric tons per hectare)
- More than 5.7 (12.7)
- 5.7 (12.7) or less
- 0

*Not all roots and tubers shown

ICELAND

UNITED KINGDOM

IRELAND (EIRE)

NORWAY

SWEDEN

FINLAND

DENMARK

NETH.

BELGIUM

LUXEMBOURG

FRANCE

ANDORRA

PORTUGAL

SPAIN

Atlantic Ocean

Bay of Biscay

North Sea

Baltic Sea

Barents Sea

RUSSIA

ESTONIA

LATVIA

LITHUANIA

RUSSIA

POLAND

BELARUS

GERMANY

LIECHTENSTEIN

SWITZ.

ITALY

SAN MARINO

MONACO

MALTA

VATICAN CITY

CZECHIA (CZECH REP.)

AUSTRIA

SLOVENIA

SLOVAKIA

HUNGARY

CROATIA

BOSNIA & HERZEGOVINA

MONTENEGRO

SERBIA

KOSOVO

ALBANIA

NORTH MACEDONIA

GREECE

BULGARIA

ROMANIA

MOLDOVA

UKRAINE

KAZAKHSTAN

GEORGIA

AZERBAIJAN

Caspian Sea

Black Sea

TURKEY

CYPRUS

ASIA

Mediterranean Sea

AFRICA

5 SARMA
North Macedonia

Pickled cabbage leaves come in handy as the outer wrappers for sarma. The leaves are filled with chopped vegetables, rice, onions, paprika, and ground meat and rolled up. The filled cabbage rolls are covered with water and cooked for a couple of hours. Eat these with a dollop of fresh yogurt on top.

3 BORSCHT
Ukraine

There are many varieties of Ukrainian borscht, a red and often sour soup made from beets, cabbage, potatoes, tomatoes, carrots, onions, garlic, dill, and other ingredients. Borscht is popular across Eastern Europe and Russia.

4 TRUFFLES
France

Truffles are not plants—and chocolate truffles are something else altogether. Wild truffles are a delicious fungus. Truffle hunters in France and Italy use dogs or pigs to root them out of the ground in the forests where they grow. Truffles are sliced and eaten raw or put in pâtés, or lightly cooked and eaten alongside eggs.

55

5 COOL FOODS

1 SZARLOTKA
Poland

Polish apple cake, szarlotka, has a crumbly top and a shortbread-like base, with plenty of fresh apples and cinnamon in between. Poland is Europe's largest apple producer.

2 RÅRÖRDA LINGON
Sweden

Lingonberries grow wild in Scandinavia and parts of Russia. They taste sour and tart, like cranberries. In Sweden, raw lingonberries stirred with a little sugar—rårörda lingon—are a tasty treat.

DIGITAL TRAVELER!

Find out how olive oil is made in the olive-growing regions of Greece, Italy, Spain, and Portugal. Many facilities that press the olives to produce olive oil offer fun tours and tastings.

FRUIT PRODUCTION*
U.S. tons per acre
(metric tons per hectare)

- More than 10.7 (24)
- 10.7 (24) or less
- 0

*Not all fruits shown

ICELAND

Norwegian Sea

Barents Sea

SWEDEN

FINLAND

NORWAY

UNITED KINGDOM

North Sea

ESTONIA

LATVIA

RUSSIA

LITHUANIA

RUSSIA

Atlantic Ocean

IRELAND (ÉIRE)

DENMARK

NETH.

BELGIUM

GERMANY

LUXEMBOURG

POLAND

BELARUS

KAZAKHSTAN

Bay of Biscay

FRANCE

LIECHTENSTEIN

SWITZ.

CZECHIA (CZECH REP.)

SLOVAKIA

UKRAINE

AUSTRIA

HUNGARY

MOLDOVA

Caspian Sea

PORTUGAL

ANDORRA

SLOVENIA

ITALY

CROATIA

ROMANIA

SPAIN

MONACO

SAN MARINO

BOSNIA & HERZEGOVINA

SERBIA

GEORGIA

AZERBAIJAN

Black Sea

MONTENEGRO

KOSOVO

BULGARIA

VATICAN CITY

NORTH MACEDONIA

TURKEY

ALBANIA

GREECE

ASIA

Mediterranean Sea

MALTA

CYPRUS

3 ORANGE MARMALADE
Spain

Orange trees grow along the streets of Seville, Spain. But don't eat their fruits! Seville oranges are bitter, which makes them just right for marmalade. The bitter oranges are boiled with sugar and a lemon or two.

PEELS AND PODS

Juicy FRUITS, crunchy nuts, and hearty BEANS

a fruit and vegetable market stall in Germany

EUROPE

Fruits grown and commonly eaten in Europe include apples, pears, grapes, melons, olives, bananas, and lingonberries. The Mediterranean countries are home to citrus groves and fig trees, which grow well in the warm, sunny climate. Cherries and strawberries, on the other hand, grow as far north as Scandinavia. Walnuts from trees in France, Romania, and parts of southern Europe are used in many dishes. Common European legumes—plants that produce seeds in pods—are peas, green beans, chickpeas, and lentils.

APPETIZING ATTRACTIONS

CHOCOLATE FACTORY

Visit Cadbury World in Birmingham, England, to learn about the history of chocolate and how it's made, taste samples, and even try to make your own chocolate. A factory here inspired British author Roald Dahl to write the book *Charlie and the Chocolate Factory*.

4 LENTIL SOUP
Turkey

Lentils are eaten throughout Europe, but especially around the Mediterranean. This red lentil soup from Turkey, part of which lies in Europe, is made with split red lentils, potatoes, carrots, onions, garlic, and other vegetables and seasonings.

PICK UP TOMATOES

Tomatoes need warm sunshine, but some smart folks in Sweden figured out how to raise them in far northern Europe. More than 80 varieties of tasty tomatoes grow in Vikentomater's greenhouses, and you can visit and buy fresh-picked tomatoes there. They plant seeds in December and harvest from March through November.

CHESTNUT FESTIVAL

Look for chestnut trees in southern France. Farmers there have grown chestnut trees—sometimes called bread trees—for centuries. In late autumn, eat marrons glacés—candied chestnuts—at Castagnades, a festival in Ardeche.

5 ESCUDELLA
Andorra

People in the small country of Andorra, high in the Pyrenees mountains, enjoy a hearty soup called escudella. To make it, white beans are cooked and then added to vegetables, pasta, and meats that may include local wild boar or rabbit.

STRANGE BUT TRUE

Although bananas grow mostly in the warmer climates of South America, Asia, and Africa, they're also produced in Europe. Spain, Italy, and Greece grow some. More surprisingly, they're also cultivated even farther north—in Iceland! (In heated greenhouses, of course.)

FULL OF FLAVOR

harvest fruits

DIGITAL TRAVELER!
Find out what, when, and where the Csabai Kolbászfesztivál is. Hint: It involves the Hungarian Csaba sausage. Compare it with the Lincoln Sausage Festival in the United Kingdom.

Delicious DELIGHTS through the YEAR

Let's celebrate! Since ancient times, people have celebrated food with festivals, giving thanks to their God or gods for the harvest of the fields and seas. Today's food festivals run the gamut from the serious to the silly. You'll find competitions to judge whose produce is the finest, and who can eat the fastest. You can learn about how foods are produced and how to prepare local ingredients. But above all, food festivals encourage visitors to have fun and enjoy a meal.

1 CHERRY FESTIVAL
Bulgaria

Kyustendil, known as the Fruit Garden of Bulgaria, hosts a two-day cherry festival in June. Visitors can taste different cherry varieties, drink cherry kompot, and eat foods made with cherries. There are prizes for the largest cherry and for the best sculpture made from cherries.

2 PIEROGI FESTIVAL
Poland

Pierogi are hot dumplings stuffed with sweet or savory fillings. They're popular throughout Eastern Europe, but especially in Poland. Each summer, people gather in Kraków to celebrate this dish. Stalls sell many varieties of pierogi, and there is a "best pierogi" contest. The festival also includes traditional folk music and folk art.

5 COOL FOOD EVENTS

① Bulgaria
② Poland
③ Sweden
④ Malta
⑤ Switzerland

3 NORDIC OYSTER OPENING FESTIVAL
Sweden

In this springtime event, Scandinavia's best oyster openers race to see who can open 30 oysters in the shortest time. Spectators can cheer the champions and taste a variety of very fresh oysters and other seafoods.

EUROPE

4 CHOCOLATE FESTIVAL
Malta

Enjoy the sweet warmth of late October. In Hamrun, Malta, you'll find the streets filled with people, music, and chocolate: brownies, cookies, hot cocoa, and other delicious treats.

5 ZIBELEMÄRIT
Switzerland

Your nose will know—this is a festival of onions and garlic! In late November in Bern, farmers bring their produce to town, often braided into artistic shapes and figures. Be sure to look for the "Onion Heads" at this celebration. They're people wearing masks who parade and sing through the town.

TRY THIS RECIPE
CHERRY KOMPOT
A TASTE OF BULGARIA

Kompot is a sweet drink popular throughout Eastern Europe. This version is made with cherries, but it can be made with other fruit. It can be served hot or cold.

Prep time: 5 minutes for frozen cherries, 20 minutes for fresh cherries
Serves: 6 people

1½ pounds (about 4 cups) fresh or frozen cherries
6 cups water
6 tablespoons sugar
3 tablespoons lemon juice

① If using fresh cherries, wash them and remove the stems. Have an adult help you remove the pits. Set the cherries aside.
② Pour the water and sugar into a large pot. With an adult's help, bring the mixture to a boil over high heat.
③ Reduce heat to medium-high.
④ Carefully add the fresh or frozen cherries and lemon juice to the hot water. Bring back to a boil for 5 minutes.
⑤ Turn off the stove. Remove the pot from the heat, cover, and let the kompot cool for at least 30 minutes.
⑥ Serve the kompot hot or cold, with or without cherries.

5 **COOL FOODS**

CHURROS CON CHOCOLATE

Look for a churreria in Spain or Portugal to find churros—long sticks of fried dough that you can dip into hot chocolate for a breakfast treat.

HESSENPARK

This open-air museum in Neu-Anspach, Hesse, Germany, stores and grows heritage grains—older seed varieties from the past that are being grown again today. It also has historical buildings that have been restored, including an inn where you can sample local meals.

TRDELNÍK

In Prague, Czechia (Czech Republic), look for street vendors preparing this tasty treat. Pastry dough is wrapped around a stick and roasted over an open flame, then dusted with cinnamon or sugar.

DIGITAL TRAVELER!
In Greece, phyllo pastry is used widely. *Phyllo* means "leaf" in Greek. Find out how the pastry got its name.

1 HAGGIS
United Kingdom

Oatmeal is a key ingredient in making the Scottish specialty haggis. The oatmeal is mixed together with ground-up meats and seasonings, then stuffed into the stomach of a sheep or calf. Fans of haggis say it's savory and delicious.

GRAIN PRODUCTION*
U.S. tons per acre
(metric tons per hectare)

■	More than 0.1 (0.3)
■	0.1 (0.3) or less
□	0

*Not all grains shown

2 BLACK RYE BREAD
Latvia

Black rye bread is popular in Latvia. For a breakfast snack, try it with butter, tomato, and onion slices. For dessert, try rupjmaizes kārtojums—pieces of black rye bread with cranberries and whipped cream.

3 PASTA AND CHICKPEAS
San Marino

Pasta e ceci is a traditional dinner soup in the tiny nation of San Marino. To make the sauce for this dish, chickpeas are mashed with garlic, onions, and other seasonings. The pasta is cooked in the sauce until ready.

? **DID YOU KNOW?**

The original veggie burger—made with oats, soy, wheat gluten, and sesame—was invented in the United Kingdom in the 1970s and was first sold commercially in 1982.

ICELAND

UNITED KINGDOM
IRELAND (ÉIRE)
North Sea

Atlantic Ocean

BELGIUM

Bay of Biscay

FRANCE

PORTUGAL

ANDORRA

SPAIN

Med

AFRICA

Danish pastries and other baked goods

BEYOND BREAKFAST

CEREALS are not just for MORNING meals

EUROPE

4 DANISH PASTRIES
Denmark

Danish pastries were originally made by pastry chefs from Vienna, Austria, who brought them to Denmark. That's why in Denmark they are called *wienerbrød*, meaning "Vienna bread." These flaky treats are still made in Denmark today. The dough is folded over and filled with various jams or creams.

G rains, or kernels, are the edible seeds of certain plants that include the grasses known as cereals. They're ground up to make flour. And flour is the foundation for baking— breads, pastries, cakes, and more. Pasta, too! This makes grains important crops. Europe's most commonly grown grains are wheat and spelt (a grain related to wheat), as well as barley, corn, and some rye and rice. The biggest wheat-growing countries in Europe are Russia and France. They grow mostly winter wheat—seeds are planted in the fall and start to grow again in spring, then are harvested the following August.

5 FLIJA
Kosovo

This special dish, very popular in Kosovo, is made with simple ingredients: mainly flour, water, and salt. Layers of the pancake-like batter are slowly cooked, covered with a round metal lid topped with hot cinders, and filled with a yogurt filling. It's a pancake pie!

Barents Sea

Norwegian Sea

SWEDEN

FINLAND

NORWAY

DENMARK

ESTONIA

Baltic Sea

LATVIA

LITHUANIA

RUSSIA

RUSSIA

BELARUS

NETH.

GERMANY

LUXEMBOURG

LIECHTENSTEIN

SWITZ.

CZECHIA (CZECH REP.)

AUSTRIA

SLOVAKIA

POLAND

UKRAINE

MOLDOVA

KAZAKHSTAN

Caspian Sea

MONACO

SLOVENIA

HUNGARY

ROMANIA

SAN MARINO

CROATIA

BOSNIA & HERZEGOVINA

SERBIA

GEORGIA

AZERBAIJAN

Black Sea

ITALY

VATICAN CITY

MONTENEGRO

KOSOVO

ALBANIA

BULGARIA

NORTH MACEDONIA

TURKEY

GREECE

ASIA

ASIA

terranean Sea

MALTA

CYPRUS

LOCAL PICKS

From simple ROASTS to hearty STEWS

E uropean livestock is similar to American animals raised for their meat—so you'll see plenty of beef and lamb. But you'll notice local flavors, too. For example, goat meat is available in many countries, and in Scandinavia, where reindeer are herded, reindeer meatballs or stew may appear on the menu. In Spain, pork is so popular that in 2018, pigs outnumbered people—50 million to 46.5 million. Meanwhile in Germany, goose is favored over turkey for festive dinners.

a platter of charcuterie, or cured meats, served with olives

DIGITAL TRAVELER!

A smörgåsbord is a Scandinavian meal of Swedish origin that consists of an array of open sandwiches. It is served as a buffet, for lunch or dinner. Find out the range of meats and poultry foods used for a smörgåsbord.

APPETIZING ATTRACTIONS

▶ LEAULT WORKING SHEEPDOGS

For centuries, shepherds have relied on sheepdogs to help guard and herd their flocks. The folks on Leault Farm in Kincraig, in the Scottish Highlands, offer demonstrations of how their dogs respond to signals and control the sheep, which are kept for their meat and milk. Visitors can take a turn at shearing sheep.

▶ 3 KIDS GOAT FARM

This family farm in Romania raises goats, pigs, chickens, turkeys, ducks, and geese. It accepts international volunteers to help work on the farm, and is open to visitors looking to try some traditional Romanian farm cuisine.

▶ SNAIL FARMS

Farmers in France breed snails and raise them for escargot, a French specialty usually cooked with garlic butter and wine. There's a snail farm in Maniquerville, Normandy, where visitors can peek in at the miniature livestock and learn about the snail's life cycle.

COOL FOODS

5

2 FINNBIFF
Norway

Norwegian reindeer stew uses the meat of locally raised reindeer cooked with bacon, mushrooms, juniper berries, and other flavorings for a rich, warming meal.

1 WÜRSTE
Germany

Almost every region of Germany has its own sausage, or würst. Bratwürst and weisswürst are made from pork and veal. Other types are made from beef and venison, and there are vegan varieties. The sausages are usually served with sauerkraut—fermented raw cabbage—or potatoes.

3 SATSIVI
Georgia

In rural Georgia, keeping chickens at home ensures a good supply of fresh eggs. And of course, when visitors arrive, a good host chooses the finest chicken to prepare for a special dish, perhaps satsivi—chicken with pomegranate and walnuts.

STRANGE BUT TRUE

"Head cheese" is not a dairy product, but rather jellied meat. Called *schwartenmagen* in German, it contains various animal parts, seasoned and bound together with gelatin. It's served sliced, often in sandwiches.

CATTLE PRODUCTION
Number per square mile
(number per square kilometer)
- More than 129 (50)
- 129 (50) or less
- 0

4 JAMÓN IBÉRICO
Spain

This delicacy is a special cured ham that comes only from Iberian pigs raised in Spain. All over Spain you can spot entire ham legs hanging from the ceilings of restaurants, cafés, and shops. Families purchase a leg to keep on a counter at home, carefully shaving off a fresh serving as needed.

5 KLEFTIKO
Greece

With a goat population of almost four million, Greece is a great place to taste goat kleftiko. The meat is slow-baked on the bone. Traditionally, this was done in a pit oven. It's said that this method was used long ago by klephts, or rural thieves, who would steal a goat and roast it in a sealed pit to hide the smoke and avoid getting caught.

CREAMY CRAVINGS

Making the most of MILK

Dairy is a category of foods made from the milk of farm animals, such as cows, sheep, goats, and water buffalo. Dairy products are important in many European meals, from milk in breakfast cereal to butter on toast to yogurt or ice cream for dessert. Germany, France, Switzerland, and the United Kingdom all have large dairy herds. French cheeses and yogurts are famous worldwide.

an ice-cream tower

1 SKYR
Iceland

Skyr is a soft, liquidy cheese from Iceland with the consistency of a yogurt. It's made from skim milk, so it's nonfat and nutritious. It is often served as a dessert, sometimes with cream or fresh berries.

5 COOL FOODS

2 SPAGHETTIEIS
Germany

Is that spaghetti or ice cream? This dish, which was invented by the son of an Italian immigrant, is served all over Germany. It's made by pressing vanilla or other light-colored ice cream through a potato ricer or similar tool to make "noodles." Strawberry sauce and white chocolate shavings complete the look.

3 KEFIR
Russia

This sour drink was first created in the Caucasus Mountains of Russia. A special combination of bacteria and yeasts is added to cow's or goat's milk. Kefir is said to be good for maintaining health.

1 ICELAND

UNITED KINGDOM

IRELAND (ÉIRE)

North Sea

BELGIUM

Atlantic Ocean

Bay of Biscay

FRANCE

PORTUGAL

ANDORRA

SPAIN

Med

AFRICA

4 BUTTER
Luxembourg

All butter is not alike. European butters are richer than American butter because they are churned longer to produce more butterfat. Europeans even designate certain butters as originating in a specific area: Luxembourg's "Beurre Rose" label can be used only on butter from that tiny country.

THICK YOGURT
Greek yogurt is prepared in a special way so that is it thicker and more flavorful than other types of yogurt. At Stani Milk Shop in Athens, Greece, order a dish of thick Greek yogurt made from sheep's milk from nearby farms. It's traditionally served with a topping of honey and chopped walnuts.

CHEESE MUSEUM
At the Amsterdam Cheese Museum, discover the history of cheese and how it is made. You can dress up as a traditional Dutch cheese farmer, and taste cheeses including Gouda, one of the country's most famous varieties.

GELATERIAS
In Italy there are about 37,000 gelaterias—shops selling gelato, that delicious, creamy, milk-based Italian ice cream. Try flavors such as coconut cream, fig, or chocolate with hazelnut.

EUROPE

DIGITAL TRAVELER!
Some say Thomas Jefferson, not Italians, invented macaroni and cheese. Find out what is known (and not known) about the origins of mac and cheese.

MILK PRODUCTION
U.S. tons per acre
(metric tons per hectare)
- More than 0.1 (0.2)
- 0.02–0.1 (0.05–0.2)
- 0.01–0.02 (0.03–0.05)
- 0.004–0.009 (0.01–0.02)
- Less than 0.004 (0.01)
- No data

5 FRIKA
Slovenia

Frika is made from grated Tolminc cheese fried in fat, with various combinations of bacon, potato, egg, cottage cheese, or meat added. In Slovenia's Soca Valley, frika is cooked on an open wood fire, giving it a rich, smoky flavor. Each village in the valley has a different recipe.

Barents Sea

Norwegian Sea

SWEDEN
NORWAY
FINLAND
DENMARK
Baltic Sea
ESTONIA
LATVIA
LITHUANIA
RUSSIA
NETH.
GERMANY
LUXEMBOURG
LIECHTENSTEIN
CZECHIA (CZECH REP.)
SLOVAKIA
SWITZ.
AUSTRIA
MONACO
SLOVENIA
CROATIA
HUNGARY
SAN MARINO
BOSNIA & HERZEGOVINA
SERBIA
MONTENEGRO
ITALY
VATICAN CITY
KOSOVO
ALBANIA
NORTH MACEDONIA
BULGARIA
ROMANIA
MOLDOVA
UKRAINE
BELARUS
POLAND
RUSSIA
KAZAKHSTAN
GEORGIA
AZERBAIJAN
Caspian Sea
Black Sea
TURKEY
GREECE
ASIA
Mediterranean Sea
MALTA
CYPRUS

ASIA

DID YOU KNOW?
Hot chocolate drinks are a popular dairy product in Europe. In cafés, hot chocolates are thick and velvety—like drinking a melted chocolate bar. Café Angelina in Paris serves a particularly thick version along with fresh whipped cream.

FEASTS OF FISH

herring and mackerel caught from the Atlantic

Sole, SPRAT, soup, and SQUID

Europeans enjoy a wealth of food from the sea and freshwater lakes and rivers. From the northern fisheries of the Norwegian Sea and North Sea to the Mediterranean, fishing boats bring in hauls of herring, salmon, trout, mackerel, sole, swordfish, and more. However, overfishing, climate change, and water pollution have reduced many fish populations. Europeans have begun to rely more on aquaculture to increase seafood production and ease stress on wild populations. Farmers raise shellfish like mussels and oysters; fish including salmon, seabream, and seabass; and even algae on their fish farms.

APPETIZING ATTRACTIONS

➥ FISH MARKET
The busy Bergen Fish Market in Bergen, Norway, dates from the 1200s. It is located in the heart of the city, which is surrounded by mountains and fjords. The vendors there sell not only fresh fish and shellfish, but also fruits, vegetables, and flowers.

➥ SEA OF FISH RESTAURANTS
Ayia Napa, a resort area of Cyprus, has long been home to many fishers. Watch them bring in their catches and then sample their fish at one of the many seafood restaurants that line the beach.

➥ LAKE SKADAR
To enjoy the beauty of a pristine natural park, and perhaps also snag some extremely fresh lake carp, check out Lake Skadar. The largest lake in southern Europe, it's on the border between Montenegro and Albania, and is home to more than 50 species of fish and 270 bird species. Fresh-caught carp is served in small local restaurants, often deep fried in hot oil.

5 COOL FOODS

1 CRNI RIŽOT
Croatia

This black-colored rice and seafood dish is a risotto made with cuttlefish or squid, often with other seafood mixed in. The addition of ink from the squid or cuttlefish turns the dish a deep black and gives it a rich flavor.

2 SPRAT SANDWICH
Estonia

A sprat is a small fish that's plentiful in the Baltic Sea off the coast of Estonia. Sprat sandwiches are popular here, usually served open-faced on dark bread with cheese and parsley or a hard-boiled egg and chives.

! STRANGE BUT TRUE
"Irish Moss" isn't moss; it's the name of a seaweed. In Ireland, people use it to make a paste to thicken pies and desserts.

3 FISH-AND-CHIPS
United Kingdom

Fried battered whitefish and french fries come together in this popular British dish. It's often served at take-out restaurants. A pickled onion is a popular addition. Traditionally, fish-and-chips were sprinkled with salt and vinegar and served in a newspaper cone, but newspaper wrappers aren't used much anymore.

DIGITAL TRAVELER!
The 16th-century Italian painter Giuseppe Arcimboldo created portraits using depictions of fruits, vegetables, flowers, and fish to form human faces. Find examples of his work and look for food paintings by other famous artists.

EUROPE

AMOUNT OF FISH CAUGHT
Average pounds (kilograms) per person per year

- More than 132 (60)
- 68–132 (31–60)
- 46–67 (21–30)
- 11–45 (5–20)
- Less than 11 (5)

Barents Sea

ICELAND

Norwegian Sea

SWEDEN

FINLAND

NORWAY

Baltic Sea

RUSSIA

2 ESTONIA

LATVIA

LITHUANIA

RUSSIA

BELARUS

IRELAND (ÉIRE)

UNITED KINGDOM

3 DENMARK

NETH.

Atlantic Ocean

BELGIUM

GERMANY

POLAND

LUXEMBOURG

CZECHIA (CZECH REP.)

SLOVAKIA

UKRAINE

Bay of Biscay

LIECHTENSTEIN

AUSTRIA

SWITZ.

HUNGARY

MOLDOVA

FRANCE

SLOVENIA

ROMANIA

MONACO

5

CROATIA

1

KAZAKHSTAN

Caspian Sea

GEORGIA

AZERBAIJAN

PORTUGAL

4

ANDORRA

SAN MARINO

BOSNIA & HERZEGOVINA

SERBIA

MONTENEGRO

BULGARIA

Black Sea

SPAIN

ITALY

VATICAN CITY

KOSOVO

NORTH MACEDONIA

ALBANIA

TURKEY

ASIA

GREECE

Mediterranean Sea

AFRICA

MALTA

CYPRUS

5 BOUILLABAISSE
Monaco

Located on the Mediterranean Sea, the small country of Monaco borrows much of its cuisine from France, which surrounds it. Many restaurants here serve bouillabaisse, a classic soup made from clams, lobster, and fish in a delicately flavored broth.

4 BACALHAU
Portugal

The Portuguese say they eat cod, or bacalhau, prepared 1,000 different ways! The fish can be salted, baked, fried, breaded, rolled into balls, and served in cream sauce. Each region of the country has its own bacalhau recipes and choices of side dishes.

SAY "CHEESE"!

a selection of cheeses

5 COOL FOODS

CHEESES around the WORLD

Cheese is made from milk that has been treated to form lumps known as curds. The curds are squeezed together to make the soft or hard masses we call cheese. Nobody knows who first made and ate cheese, but it was popular among ancient Romans and became a widespread staple throughout their empire. The top cheese-eating countries are in Europe, but cheese is popular around the world. People make cheese from the milk of many animals—usually cows, but often sheep and goats, and less often buffalo, camels, and even moose.

1 PIZZA
United States

Where there's cheese, there's pizza! Italy is credited with its invention, but Italian immigrants in New York made pizza an American favorite. U.S. pizzas go beyond the traditional mozzarella and tomato, using different cheese mixes and creative toppings, including pineapple and broccoli.

TRUE OR FALSE?

Which of these statements about cheese or milk are true and which are false?

1. Yak cheese (made from yak milk) is popular in Nepal.
2. One pound (453 g) of milk will make one pound of cheese.
3. In Europe, South America, and Asia, many stores sell milk that, if unopened, stays fresh on the shelf for months—even if it's not refrigerated.
4. The world record for the largest pizza ever made is held by a team of Italians who created a pizza bigger than the surface area of an Olympic swimming pool.
5. People in South Africa eat less cheese on average than people in any other country.

2 CATUPIRY
Brazil

This soft cheese from Brazil is popular throughout the country. It is even served as a dessert, with guava paste—a treat sometimes called Romeo and Julieta.

See answers on page 150.

3 AYIB
Ethiopia

Ayib is a moist, mild cheese similar to cottage cheese. It goes well with the bold, spicy flavors of much Ethiopian cooking—alongside kitfo (raw beef) and lentils and herbs. Try a blob of this soft cheese on top of a spicy lentil stew.

DIGITAL TRAVELER!
Raclette is a Swiss cheese that is served melted. In the old days, shepherds would melt the cheese on a heated stone, scraping off the softened part as it warmed. Find out how raclette is prepared and eaten today.

Arctic Ocean

NORTH AMERICA

Pacific Ocean

Atlantic Ocean

EUROPE

ASIA

AFRICA

Pacific Ocean

Indian Ocean

SOUTH AMERICA

AUSTRALIA

ANTARCTICA

CHEESE PRODUCTION
Pounds per person
(kilograms per person)
- More than 4.4 (2)
- 4.4 (2) or less
- 0

5 CHEDDAR AND BEEF PIE
New Zealand

New Zealand cheesemakers use many techniques borrowed from Europe to make a range of cheeses. Cheese is often baked into the country's popular hand pies—small, warm pastries filled with meats and a combination of other ingredients. A favorite combo is beef and cheddar.

4 PANEER
India

Many Indian recipes rely on this cheese, and it's easy to make paneer at home. Just heat milk and add lemon juice or vinegar. Paneer can be crumbled or cubed, and it doesn't melt, so it can be put on a skewer and grilled with vegetables.

ASIA

VARIED cuisines bursting with FLAVOR

As the largest continent in both area and population, Asia boasts a huge range of foods. In East Asia, common foods include rice, noodles, chicken, and plenty of vegetables. In South Asia, people enjoy rice, fish, chicken, insects, seaweed, flatbreads, and curries and other spices. Southeast Asia, which includes many islands, features tropical fruits. Western Asia, which is a region of deserts surrounded by seas, has a menu rich in fruits, legumes, herbs, and spices. Central Asia lies to the north in the mountains west of China, and its cuisine is shaped by the nomadic traditions of its people. What a variety!

This street market in Malaysia offers many different skewered meats and vegetables with dipping sauces.

FOODIE HOT SPOTS

 GROWING RICE

Rice is a part of meals across Asia, and is grown even on hillside terraces.

 LEMONGRASS

In Laos, fresh lemongrass is a key ingredient to flavor soups, teas, curries, and stir-fries.

 KUMQUAT

This grape-size citrus fruit native to eastern Asia has sour flesh and a sweet rind.

 RICE DISH FESTIVAL

In January, Tamil Hindus in Sri Lanka thank their sun god, Surya, for the rice harvest.

 LAVASH BREAD

In Armenia, try lavash—a speckled, puffy, flexible bread used to scoop up other foods.

 SPICY SATAY

In Indonesia, pieces of tender chicken are grilled and doused in a spicy peanut sauce.

 AARUUL

Aaruul is a dried cheese from Mongolia that is often sweetened with fruit and sugar.

 RAW FISH SNACK

In Japan, try sashimi, which is thinly sliced raw meat or fish eaten with soy sauce.

 A SUGARY WORLD

Russia produces vast amounts of sugar to sweeten foods and drinks.

FAST FACTS

Size ranking: The largest
Number of countries: 46 (excluding Russia)
Total population: 4,402,007,000
Largest country by area: China

Arctic Ocean

A commonly accepted division between Asia and Europe is formed by the Ural Mountains, Ural River, Caspian Sea, Caucasus Mountains, and the Black Sea with its outlets to the Aegean Sea, the Bosporus, and the Dardanelles. A large part of Russia lies in Asia.

EUROPE

RUSSIA

Mediterranean Sea

Ankara
TURKEY
GEORGIA ⊕ Tbilisi
ARMENIA
LEBANON Beirut ⊕ Yerevan ⊕ **AZERBAIJAN**
Jerusalem ⊕ **SYRIA** ⊕ Baku
ISRAEL ⊕ Damascus
JORDAN Amman ⊕ **TURKMENISTAN**
Baghdad ⊕ Tehran ⊕ Ashgabat
IRAQ
SAUDI Kuwait ⊕ **IRAN**
ARABIA City
⊕ **KUWAIT**
Riyadh ⊕ **BAHRAIN** ⊕ Manama
⊕ **QATAR** Doha
UNITED ARAB ⊕ Abu Dhabi
EMIRATES ⊕ Muscat
Sanaa ⊕
YEMEN
OMAN

AFRICA

Arabian Sea

Nur-Sultan ⊕
KAZAKHSTAN

Ulaanbaatar ⊕
MONGOLIA

Bishkek ⊕
UZBEKISTAN
Tashkent ⊕ **KYRGYZSTAN**
⊕ Dushanbe
TAJIKISTAN
Kabul ⊕ Islamabad ⊕
AFGHANISTAN

Beijing ⊕

CHINA

PAKISTAN New ⊕
Delhi
NEPAL **BHUTAN**
Kathmandu ⊕ ⊕ Thimphu
BANGLADESH
Dhaka ⊕ **MYANMAR**
(BURMA)
INDIA Nay Pyi Taw ⊕ **LAOS** Hanoi ⊕
⊕ Vientiane
THAILAND **VIETNAM**
Bangkok ⊕ ⊕ **CAMBODIA**
Phnom ⊕
Penh

NORTH
KOREA
Pyongyang ⊕ **JAPAN**
Tokyo ⊕
Seoul ⊕
SOUTH
KOREA

Taipei ⊕
TAIWAN

South
China
Sea

Manila ⊕
PHILIPPINES

Pacific
Ocean

The People's Republic of China claims Taiwan as its 23rd province. Taiwan maintains that there are two political entities.

Bay of
Bengal

Colombo ⊕
Male ⊕ **SRI LANKA**
⊕ **MALDIVES**

Indian Ocean

Kuala Lumpur ⊕
⊕ **SINGAPORE**
MALAYSIA

BRUNEI
Bandar Seri
Begawan ⊕

INDONESIA

Jakarta ⊕
Java Sea

Dili ⊕
TIMOR-LESTE
(EAST TIMOR)

POLITICAL MAP
⊕ National capital
⊙ Other capital

0 ——— 800 miles
0 ——— 800 kilometers

ASIA

AUNT BERTHA'S FOOD TRAVEL TIPS

* Grab a meal or snack at a food stall where local people are eating. If the food is selling quickly, it's probably tasty!

* Many hotels in Asia serve guests breakfast. Skip the Western-style breakfast and go for what the locals eat. You might just find a new favorite food when you venture out to try new things.

* If you haven't eaten with chopsticks before, give it a try. Hold two chopsticks pointing in the same direction. Keep one steady between your thumb and index finger. Move the other to pinch the food.

FARMING FOR FOOD

ANCIENT TRADITIONS

From SPICY PEPPERS to YAKS and STAR FRUIT

The ancient peoples of the Fertile Crescent—parts of Syria, Iraq, and Iran—started farming many thousands of years ago. Today in much of Asia, agriculture is still carried on by family farmers. Rice is a staple—a foundation of the diet—for most Asians. Other agricultural products of this enormous continent include wheat and other grains, many vegetables, and a wide variety of fruits. Livestock animals range from ducks kept in homes to yaks and horses tended by northern nomads.

an Arctic Russian reindeer herder

APPETIZING ATTRACTIONS

➡ **BANAUE RICE TERRACES**
More than 2,000 years ago in Luzon, Philippines, the indigenous Ifugao people dug a vast system of irrigated rice terraces. Still used for growing rice, the terraces are a giant staircase of watery green fields.

➡ **NATIONAL SCENIC AREA**
Travelers to Taiwan can visit one of many major farming areas at Siraya. The scenic area is divided into 16 districts. Each one specializes in growing certain fruits and vegetables, from avocados to papayas. Check out the mango and coffee plantations.

➡ **VISIT A KIBBUTZ**
A kibbutz in Israel is a special farming community where everyone lives together and shares in the work, such as caring for animals, sowing seeds, picking fruits, and cooking. Volunteers from around the world—usually aged 18 to 35—can join in to spend a few months working and learning about farming.

5 COOL FOODS

1 TARO ROOT
Malaysia

This sweet and starchy root was cultivated in Malaysia 2,000 years ago and is now grown and eaten in many Asian countries and the Pacific Islands. In Malaysia, where it's often referred to as yam, it is cooked, cut up, and served mixed with rice, onions, and spices.

2 BIBIMBAP
South Korea

In South Korea, as in many Asian nations, rice is the most important crop. A favorite meal here is *bibimbap*, meaning "mixed rice"—a hot dish or bowl of rice topped with vegetables and meat. A raw egg cracked into the bowl cooks in the sizzling dish.

DIGITAL TRAVELER!

Pomelo, a citrus fruit indigenous to South and Southeast Asia, can grow as large as a soccer ball. It is believed to be the ancestor of the grapefruit. Find out which countries pomelo is grown in today.

FARMLAND USAGE

- Pasture
- Cropland
- Other land use

Pacific Ocean

JAPAN

NORTH KOREA

2 SOUTH KOREA

TAIWAN

PHILIPPINES

VIETNAM

South China Sea

BRUNEI

1 MALAYSIA

SINGAPORE

INDONESIA

Java Sea

TIMOR-LESTE (EAST TIMOR)

CAMBODIA

THAILAND

LAOS

MYANMAR (BURMA)

Bay of Bengal

SRI LANKA

4 MALDIVES

Indian Ocean

RUSSIA

Arctic Ocean

EUROPE

MONGOLIA

CHINA

BHUTAN **3**

NEPAL

BANGLADESH

INDIA

KAZAKHSTAN **5**

UZBEKISTAN

KYRGYZSTAN

TAJIKISTAN

TURKMENISTAN

AFGHANISTAN

PAKISTAN

IRAN

Arabian Sea

AZERBAIJAN

ARMENIA

GEORGIA

TURKEY

Mediterranean Sea

LEBANON

ISRAEL

JORDAN

SYRIA

IRAQ

KUWAIT

SAUDI ARABIA

BAHRAIN →

QATAR

UNITED ARAB EMIRATES

OMAN

YEMEN

AFRICA

DID YOU KNOW?

Centuries ago in many Asian cultures, the emperor or king would mark the start of each year's farming season by plowing a field in a public ceremony.

4 STAR FRUIT
Sri Lanka

Native to Sri Lanka but now grown in other warm parts of the world, star fruit has a unique shape. When the fruit is cut across its broad side, slices are star-shaped.

3 CHEESE AND CHILIES
Bhutan

People grow many types of chili peppers in Bhutan, a country nestled between India and China. Although chilies originated in South America, the Bhutanese eat enormous quantities of the spicy peppers, claiming this helps keep them warm during cold winters. A favorite local meal is cheese and chilies, or ema datshi.

5 BESHBARMAK
Kazakhstan

Central Asia has traditionally focused on raising livestock rather than crops, and the diet there tends to be meat-based. Kazakhstan's beshbarmak, which translates to "five fingers," is a dish people usually eat with their hands, using noodles to scoop up slices or chunks of meat.

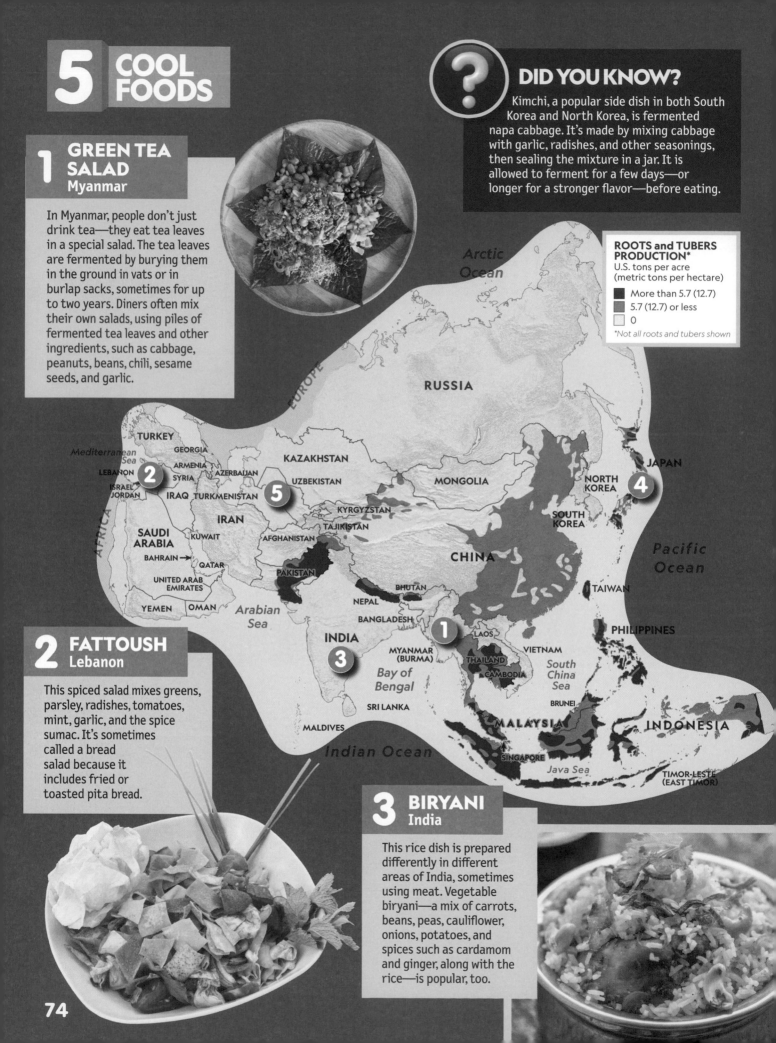

5 COOL FOODS

? DID YOU KNOW?

Kimchi, a popular side dish in both South Korea and North Korea, is fermented napa cabbage. It's made by mixing cabbage with garlic, radishes, and other seasonings, then sealing the mixture in a jar. It is allowed to ferment for a few days—or longer for a stronger flavor—before eating.

1 GREEN TEA SALAD
Myanmar

In Myanmar, people don't just drink tea—they eat tea leaves in a special salad. The tea leaves are fermented by burying them in the ground in vats or in burlap sacks, sometimes for up to two years. Diners often mix their own salads, using piles of fermented tea leaves and other ingredients, such as cabbage, peanuts, beans, chili, sesame seeds, and garlic.

ROOTS and TUBERS PRODUCTION*
U.S. tons per acre
(metric tons per hectare)

- More than 5.7 (12.7)
- 5.7 (12.7) or less
- 0

*Not all roots and tubers shown

RUSSIA

Arctic Ocean

EUROPE

Mediterranean Sea
TURKEY
GEORGIA
ARMENIA
AZERBAIJAN
LEBANON
SYRIA
ISRAEL
JORDAN
IRAQ TURKMENISTAN
KAZAKHSTAN
UZBEKISTAN
KYRGYZSTAN
TAJIKISTAN
MONGOLIA
NORTH KOREA
JAPAN
SOUTH KOREA
AFRICA
SAUDI ARABIA
KUWAIT
IRAN
AFGHANISTAN
CHINA
Pacific Ocean
BAHRAIN
QATAR
PAKISTAN
BHUTAN
TAIWAN
UNITED ARAB EMIRATES
NEPAL
YEMEN
OMAN
Arabian Sea
BANGLADESH
INDIA
MYANMAR (BURMA)
LAOS
VIETNAM
PHILIPPINES
THAILAND
CAMBODIA
South China Sea
Bay of Bengal
SRI LANKA
BRUNEI
MALDIVES
MALAYSIA
INDONESIA
SINGAPORE
Java Sea
Indian Ocean
TIMOR-LESTE (EAST TIMOR)

2 FATTOUSH
Lebanon

This spiced salad mixes greens, parsley, radishes, tomatoes, mint, garlic, and the spice sumac. It's sometimes called a bread salad because it includes fried or toasted pita bread.

3 BIRYANI
India

This rice dish is prepared differently in different areas of India, sometimes using meat. Vegetable biryani—a mix of carrots, beans, peas, cauliflower, onions, potatoes, and spices such as cardamom and ginger, along with the rice—is popular, too.

VEGGIES, ROOTS, SHOOTS

MULTI-USE PLANTS

sticky rice wrapped in banana leaves

From VEGGIE WRAPS to TEA LEAVES

A sian foods include all kinds of vegetables, from the roots of wetland plants to garden greens and food derived from the wood pulp of tree trunks. These local ingredients are prepared with seasonings and other elements that vary from place to place. Leaves have additional uses, too: Grape leaves are popular food wrappers in the Middle East, while in Southeast Asia, where banana trees grow, people make use of their leaves. By folding a leaf into a boat shape, they can use it to steam meats, spices, and eggs. Leaves are also handy to wrap dishes, such as the Malaysian breakfast rice meal of nasi lemak.

APPETIZING ATTRACTIONS

ASIA

PICK YOUR OWN
Wherever you travel, look for opportunities to pick your own vegetables. In Singapore, the possibilities include Bollywood Veggies, Green Circle Eco Farm, and Quan Fa Organic Farm.

BAMBOO FOREST
Bamboo shoots are commonly used in Asian stir-fries, soups, and other dishes. The bamboo plant is a grass, but it can grow as tall as a tree. In western Kyoto, Japan, the Sagano Bamboo Forest is a gorgeous landscape.

TIME FOR TEA
Plantations in and around Mae Salong, in northern Thailand, grow some of the world's best oolong tea. You can see the tea plants growing in the fields, and at harvest, find piles of tea leaves drying beside small tea factories.

4 LOTUS ROOT
Japan

The lotus plant, or sacred water lily is native to Asia and grows in the water with its roots in the mud. In many Asian countries, people harvest it and eat the roots and stems. In Japan, a specialty is sliced lotus root and carrot salad, with ginger, sesame seeds, sugar, and vinegar.

5 GREEN NOODLES
Uzbekistan

Cooks in Khiwa, Uzbekistan, add green to a meal by dyeing noodles bright green with fresh dill. The noodles— shivit oshi—are often topped with a beef stew and a spoonful of yogurt. Khiva was once an important stop on the Silk Road, a trade route through Asia.

DIGITAL TRAVELER!
Indigenous herbs, such as ginger, lemongrass, and sweet basil, are widely used in cooking throughout Asia. Look up the local herbs of a country you're visiting and find recipes that use them.

GRAND MIXTURE

durian fruit

 **STRANGE BUT TRUE**

The durian, highly prized in much of Asia, is considered the King of Fruits. The thorny fruit has a reputation for being stinky, but durian lovers say the ripe fruit tastes delicious, sweet, and creamy.

Nifty NUTS, fresh fruits, and LENTIL stews

The fruits and legumes of Asia are especially varied. The mountain forests of Central Asia produce wild nuts and fruits; farmers in many countries raise crops of legumes (peas, beans, soy, and lentils); and in southern Asia, tropical fruit trees offer up treasures of many shapes, sizes, and flavors.

5 COOL FOODS

1 APRICOTS
Uzbekistan

Wild apricots grow in the mountains and valleys of Uzbekistan—more than 80 varieties! Throughout Central Asia, dried apricots are a popular snack. People also add them to meat and rice dishes, or make fresh apricots into jams and preserves.

2 BABA GANOUSH
Syria

The preparation of this popular western Asian dish varies among cooks and countries, but in Syria it consists of mashed cooked eggplant with garlic, lemon, tahini, olive oil, salt, and other seasonings. It's a tasty dip for vegetables or bread.

Mediterranean Sea
TURKEY
GEORGIA
LEBANON
ARMENIA
AZERBAIJA
ISRAEL
JORDAN
2 SYRIA
TURKMENISTA
IRAQ
AFRICA
SAUDI ARABIA
IRAN
KUWAIT
BAHRAIN
QATAR
UNITED ARAB EMIRATES
YEMEN
OMAN
Arabian Sea

3 DAL
Bangladesh

Dal is popular all over South Asia. It is dried beans, peas, or lentils, simmered and seasoned, and turned into a hot, creamy, spicy stew or porridge. A Bangladeshi recipe uses lentils flavored with chili, cilantro, cumin, and black pepper.

5 TOFU
Timor-Leste

Tofu, or bean curd, is made with the milk of soybeans, a legume native to East Asia. It can be stir-fried, baked, or grilled, and is often mixed with vegetables, fish, or meats in China and elsewhere in East Asia. In Timor-Leste, you might buy thick slices of tofu served with soy sauce and topped with fried shallots.

4 WALNUTS
Kyrgyzstan

The forests of Kyrgyzstan are filled with wild walnut trees. In some communities, the residents move into tents in the forest for a month to harvest the nuts when they're ready. In Central Asia, walnuts are often eaten with dried fruit as a snack or used in dishes from salads and sauces to soups and desserts.

FRUIT PRODUCTION*
U.S. tons per acre
(metric tons per hectare)
- ■ More than 10.7 (24)
- ■ 10.7 (24) or less
- □ 0

*Not all fruits shown

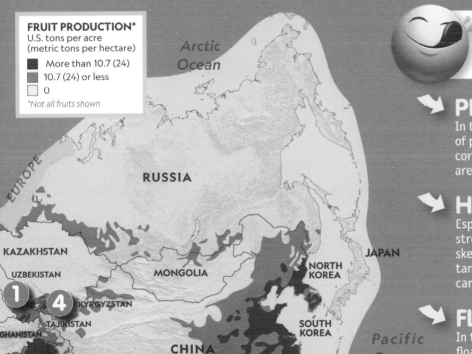

APPETIZING ATTRACTIONS

↘ **PINEAPPLE FIELDS**
In the Philippines, look for broad green acres of pineapples. Vast plantations owned by large corporations produce pineapples, many of which are canned and exported to other countries.

↘ **HAWTHORN BERRIES**
Especially around the Lunar New Year celebrations, street vendors in Chinese cities and towns sell skewers of candied Chinese hawthorn berries, called tanghulu. The candied berries look like miniature candy apples—but watch out, they're a bit sour!

↘ **FLOATING MARKET**
In the Mekong Delta of Vietnam, you'll find many floating markets. Among the busiest is Nga Nam in Soc Trang Province. People in small boats filled with fruits, vegetables, and other foods come together early in the morning to sell their wares.

DIGITAL TRAVELER!
Only a few nuts are indigenous to Japan. One is the ginkgo nut. What can you find out about this nut and how is it used in cooking?

JOYFUL TIMES

GIVING THANKS and CELEBRATING

celebrating the Hindu harvest festival of Pongal in India

Throughout Asia, people of different nationalities and religions join family and friends to celebrate their heritage on special occasions. There are special days to celebrate harvest, springtime, the new year, and even national competitions. Each festival is different, but all bring people together to celebrate and eat good food.

1 DOLMA FESTIVAL
Armenia

This May event celebrates the dolma as a matter of Armenian pride. Dolmas—grape leaves stuffed with meat, rice, and other ingredients—are a traditional Armenian dish. Participants enjoy songs and dances. The festival showcases the wide variety of dolmas (more than 60 types) and gives awards for the tastiest and longest dolma and best beginner dolma cook.

2 SAN ISIDRO PAHIYAS FESTIVAL
Philippines

At this springtime harvest fiesta in the town of Lucban, residents give thanks to Saint Isidro de Labrador, the Catholic patron saint of farmers. People create decorations with kiping (dyed rice flour wafers) for their homes, so the streets are filled with colors. Farmers bring in their fruits, vegetables, and grains and string them together with sausages called longganisa.

3 ONAM
India

During this two-week festival, the Malayali people of Kerala, India, celebrate the rice harvest. The peak event of the celebration is a Sadhya, or feast, which consists of 26 or more traditional dishes.

4 SUKKOTH
Israel

The Jewish festival of Sukkoth is a weeklong harvest celebration. In Israel, the first and last days of Sukkoth are national holidays. Throughout the world, people build sukkahs—small huts or temporary shelters—out of natural materials and hang fruits or plants inside. During the week, people eat meals in the sukkahs. Popular Sukkoth desserts are fruit compote and apple cake to symbolize a plentiful harvest.

5 COOL FOOD EVENTS

1. Armenia
2. Philippines
3. India
4. Israel
5. China

ASIA

5 MOONCAKE FESTIVAL
China

On the 15th day of the eighth month of the Chinese calendar (which usually falls in September), families gather in China, Vietnam, Singapore, and Taiwan to make offerings to the goddess of the moon, Chang'e. Mooncakes—special sweets eaten on this occasion—are made from lotus seed paste and have an egg yolk center. Children carry lighted lanterns to honor the moon.

TRY THIS RECIPE
MOONCAKES
A TASTE OF CHINA

These tasty treats are traditionally filled with lotus seed paste. You can use red bean paste instead.

Prep time: 1 hour; baking time: 15 minutes
Servings: 12 cakes

¼ cup honey
¼ cup vegetable oil
1 teaspoon baking soda
1¼ cup flour
1 cup red bean paste (chilled for at least one hour)
1 egg yolk
1 tablespoon water

1. Use a whisk to mix the honey, vegetable oil, and baking soda in a large bowl. Add flour and stir with a spoon until the dough forms a smooth ball.
2. Gently knead the dough with your hands. Cover and refrigerate for one hour.
3. While the dough is chilling, roll one tablespoon of chilled red bean paste into a ball. Make 12 balls. Refrigerate the balls until chilled.
4. Preheat the oven to 350°F.
5. Divide the chilled dough into 12 pieces. Roll each piece into a ball. Place the balls between two pieces of wax paper and flatten each ball into a thin circle.
6. Wrap each circle of dough around a red bean paste ball, fully covering the filling. Roll into a ball.
7. Place the balls on a baking sheet. Gently press each ball to flatten.
8. Beat the egg yolk and water in a small bowl with a fork. Using a basting brush, brush the mixture over the top of each cake.
9. Bake for about 15 minutes, or until golden brown.

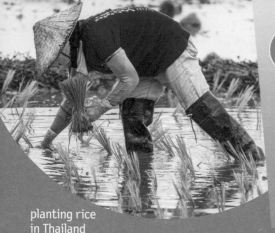
planting rice in Thailand

RICE AND MORE

TASTY noodles, breads, and TREATS

When you think of Asian foods, you probably think of rice. Indeed, Asia produces 90 percent of the world's rice. Asia grows other cereals, too, including barley, corn, sorghum, and millet. Asia's grains go into making many meals, from tasty noodles to sweet treats, from curries to fresh breads, and from stews to snacks.

5 COOL FOODS

TURKEY
Mediterranean Sea
GEORGIA
ARMENIA
LEBANON
SYRIA
AZERBAIJAN
ISRAEL
JORDAN
IRAQ
TURKMENISTAN
KUWAIT
IRAN
SAUDI ARABIA
BAHRAIN →
QATAR
UNITED ARAB EMIRATES
YEMEN
OMAN
Arabian Sea
EUROPE
KAZAKHSTAN
UZBEKISTAN
KYRGYZSTAN
TAJIKISTAN
AFGHANISTAN
PAKISTAN
INDIA
SRI LANKA
MALDIVES
AFRICA
1
2
5

GRAIN PRODUCTION*
U.S. tons per acre
(metric tons per hectare)
■ More than 0.1 (0.3)
■ 0.1 (0.3) or less
□ 0
*Not all grains shown

1 FALOODEH
Iran

Ancient Persians in the city of Shiraz invented this frozen dessert, and it's still popular today. Faloodeh is made with cooked noodles frozen in a syrup of sugar and rosewater, with a squeeze of lime. Sometimes it's topped with cherries, mint, or berries.

2 UZBEK PLOV
Uzbekistan

Plov is rice with onion and carrots, cooked slowly with lamb or beef, carefully seasoned, and often mixed with sausage and fruit. Uzbeks and neighboring people of Tajikistan prepare huge batches of plov for celebrations.

DIGITAL TRAVELER!
Asia has many kinds of breads, most of them flat. A country's traditional bread usually depends on the grains grown in the area. See how many different kinds of Asian breads you can look up and identify.

3 PORTUGUESE EGG TART
Macau

As a former colony of Portugal, Macau is an area of China where Portuguese foods are still popular. This sweet pastry has a flaky shell and a sweet egg custard filling.

4 JAJANGMYEON
South Korea

This dish is a savory mixture of noodles, fermented bean paste, vegetables, and meat or seafood. The dark bean sauce colors the noodles black. It's popular in South Korea, where you can have a bowl of jajangmyeon delivered to your door. After finishing the noodles, leave the bowl outside and the delivery person will return to collect it.

ASIA

Map labels:
Arctic Ocean
RUSSIA
MONGOLIA
JAPAN
NORTH KOREA
SOUTH KOREA
CHINA
NEPAL
BHUTAN
BANGLADESH
LAOS
TAIWAN
MYANMAR (BURMA)
THAILAND
VIETNAM
PHILIPPINES
CAMBODIA
South China Sea
Bay of Bengal
BRUNEI
MALAYSIA
INDONESIA
SINGAPORE
Java Sea
TIMOR-LESTE (EAST TIMOR)
Indian Ocean
Pacific Ocean

APPETIZING ATTRACTIONS

FRIED SNACK FORAY
In Jakarta and other Indonesian cities, street vendors with pushcarts sell gorengan—crisp and crunchy batter-fried snacks. Bakwan jagung (corn fritters) are a favorite, or try the pisang goreng (banana fritters).

DIM SUM DINING
Hong Kong is packed with restaurants serving dim sum. Originally intended as small snacks to nibble with tea, dim sum is now a major dining event. Dim sum selections such as dumplings, steamed buns, and pastries are served individually, but it's more fun if you share.

RICE CAKE MUSEUM
Tteok, a type of rice cake, is a favorite Korean food. Tteok Museum in Seoul, South Korea, runs programs for foreign visitors to show how to make tteok and kimchi, Korea's special fermented cabbage.

5 SHAHI TUKDA
Pakistan

Take some flatbread, deep fry it in ghee (clarified butter), and top it with sugar syrup—and sometimes condensed milk, dried fruits, and nuts—and you get *shahi tukda*, meaning "royal piece." It's sold on the streets of India and Pakistan and is very popular in the Pakistani city of Karachi on Eid al-Fitr, when Muslims break the month-long fast of Ramadan.

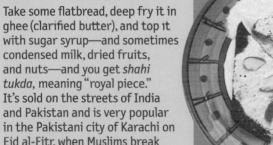

A MIX OF LIVESTOCK

From CURRIES to SOUPS and PICKLED EGGS

T hough many traditional dishes in Asia are vegetarian, Asian cuisines also feature a range of meat and poultry. In the northern and mountainous regions, yaks are well adapted to the climate and are an important food source. In Thailand and other countries, insects such as crickets are a major source of protein. Lamb, goat, and beef are also all eaten on the continent—along with preserved eggs and other poultry dishes.

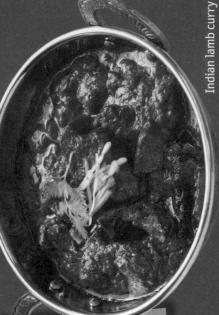

Indian lamb curry

5 COOL FOODS

1 CRICKETS
Thailand

These small creatures, traditionally raised for food in Thailand, are so nutritious that the United Nations Food and Agriculture Organization is urging more people to eat them. They provide great protein and vitamins, use fewer resources, and produce less waste than larger animals such as cows and pigs. In the city of Phuket, you can find fried crickets (and other insects) sold at restaurants and street stalls.

DID YOU KNOW?

About 80 percent of people in India and Nepal are Hindu. Cows are sacred to Hindus, and it's forbidden for them to eat beef. Cows freely wander the streets and nobody bothers them.

2 CURRIED CHICKEN
Kuwait

Quwarmah al dajaj, also known as Kuwaiti curried chicken, is a distinctive and zesty dish flavored with lime, ginger, turmeric, cumin, cinnamon, nutmeg, and other spices. It is also popular in other countries of the Middle East.

3 BEEF NOODLE SOUP
Taiwan

Beef noodle soup is considered a national dish in Taiwan. It's made with beef, Asian noodles, vegetables, and spices, including ginger, garlic, chilies, and cloves. You can eat it in noodle shops and at night markets.

DIGITAL TRAVELER!

Find out what you'd be eating if you ordered some belalang goreng or hachinoko. Restaurants in many Asian countries serve specially prepared dishes made from local insects. What other insect-based foods can you find?

4 YAK MEAT
Bhutan

Yaks are well suited to the mountainous terrain of Bhutan, where they're used for transportation, milk, and meat. One popular way to prepare yak meat to eat is to cut it into thin strips and let it dry in the air.

APPETIZING ATTRACTIONS

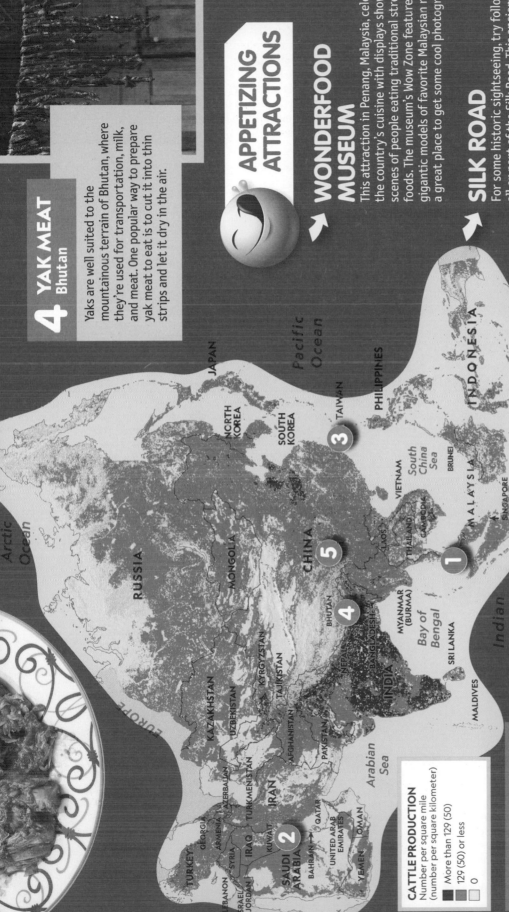

WONDERFOOD MUSEUM

This attraction in Penang, Malaysia, celebrates the country's cuisine with displays showing scenes of people eating traditional street foods. The museum's Wow Zone features gigantic models of favorite Malaysian meals. I's a great place to get some cool photographs!

SILK ROAD

For some historic sightseeing, try following all or part of the Silk Road. This ancient trade route took travelers and goods about 4,000 miles (6,437 km) from China to the Mediterranean. Along portions of the route, nomadic herders still travel with their animals, heading to new pastures throughout the year.

GHOST STREET

If you crave a late-night meal in Beijing, China, head for Guijie Street ("Ghost Street"). Red lanterns light the street all night long, and you'll find restaurants open 24/7. Popular dishes served include Peking duck, sautéed bullfrogs, and fried chicken feet.

ASIA

CATTLE PRODUCTION
Number per square mile
(number per square kilometer)

- More than 129 (50)
- 129 (50) or less
- 0

5 CENTURY EGG
China

Also called the thousand-year egg, this popular brown-and-green-colored snack is the egg of a duck, quail, or chicken that has been pickled. Raw whole eggs are soaked in a solution of lime, salt, and ash for a few weeks or months. When they're ready, you can crack open the shell and eat the insides.

Arctic Ocean

Pacific Ocean

Indian Ocean

Arabian Sea

Bay of Bengal

South China Sea

Java Sea

RUSSIA
MONGOLIA
CHINA
JAPAN
NORTH KOREA
SOUTH KOREA
TAIWAN
PHILIPPINES
INDONESIA
TIMOR-LESTE (EAST TIMOR)
VIETNAM
LAOS
THAILAND
CAMBODIA
BRUNEI
MALAYSIA
SINGAPORE
MYANMAR (BURMA)
BHUTAN
NEPAL
BANGLADESH
INDIA
SRI LANKA
MALDIVES
KAZAKHSTAN
UZBEKISTAN
KYRGYZSTAN
TAJIKISTAN
TURKMENISTAN
AFGHANISTAN
PAKISTAN
IRAN
IRAQ
KUWAIT
SAUDI ARABIA
QATAR
BAHRAIN
UNITED ARAB EMIRATES
OMAN
YEMEN
GEORGIA
ARMENIA
AZERBAIJAN
TURKEY
SYRIA
LEBANON
ISRAEL
JORDAN
EUROPE
AFRICA

5 COOL FOODS

1 GHEE
India

Butter is made from milk. When butter is heated to remove its solids, the result is ghee. Ghee, also called butter oil, is often used in cooking in the Punjabi region of India instead of other oils. It is also used in traditional medicine and for religious purposes.

2 NABULSI
West Bank

This cheese, popular in the Middle East, is named after Nablus, West Bank, the town where it originated. Made from goat's or sheep's milk, it's salty and often contains seeds that give it a spicy taste. Nabulsi is great when fried, and is also used to make a sweet cheesecake called knafeh.

MILK PRODUCTION
U.S. tons per acre
(metric tons per hectare)

- More than 0.1 (0.2)
- 0.02–0.1 (0.05–0.2)
- 0.01–0.02 (0.03–0.05)
- 0.004–0.009 (0.01–0.02)
- Less than 0.004 (0.01)
- No data

Arctic Ocean

RUSSIA

EUROPE

TURKEY
GEORGIA
Mediterranean Sea
ARMENIA
LEBANON
AZERBAIJAN
ISRAEL
SYRIA
KAZAKHSTAN
MONGOLIA
5
JAPAN
NORTH KOREA
IRAQ
TURKMENISTAN
UZBEKISTAN
2
JORDAN
KUWAIT
IRAN
KYRGYZSTAN
3
TAJIKISTAN
SOUTH KOREA
AFRICA
SAUDI ARABIA
BAHRAIN →
AFGHANISTAN
CHINA
Pacific Ocean
QATAR
PAKISTAN
1
UNITED ARAB EMIRATES
NEPAL
BHUTAN
TAIWAN
YEMEN
OMAN
BANGLADESH
Arabian Sea
INDIA
PHILIPPINES
MYANMAR (BURMA)
LAOS
VIETNAM
Bay of Bengal
THAILAND
CAMBODIA
South China Sea
SRI LANKA
BRUNEI
MALDIVES
MALAYSIA
4
INDONESIA
SINGAPORE
Indian Ocean
Java Sea
TIMOR-LESTE (EAST TIMOR)

DIGITAL TRAVELER!
Bubble tea is a chewy drink generally made of milk, ice, tea, and tapioca pearls, along with sweeteners and flavors—but sorry, no actual bubbles. Find out how and where this Asian drink got its start.

3 KURT
Turkmenistan

Since the Middle Ages, herders in Turkmenistan and throughout Central Asia have carried hard cheese balls called kurt to snack on. Families make soft cheese from the milk of cows, sheep, goats, camels, or horses, form it into balls, and dry the balls in the sun. Kurt can be eaten alone, or crumbled and added to stews, soups, or salads.

varieties of goat's cheese on sale in Turkey

MILK MARVELS

From DRINKS to CHEESES

Across Asia, people produce and eat many different dairy products. People drink the milk of animals they raise or use the milk to make foods like yogurt and ice cream. In Turkey, a soft cheese is made from goat's milk, and in Nepal people make hard cheese from yak's milk. Even in East Asia, where native people traditionally did not drink or make products from milk, dairy has become a regular part of many people's diets. In fact, China is now the world's third largest milk producer, and people there eat all sorts of dairy products.

4 AIS KACANG
Malaysia

Combine a plate full of shaved ice, ice cream, fruits, sweet corn, beans, and syrups for a cooling, flavorful, and popular Malaysian dessert. *Ais kacang* means "bean ice."

? DID YOU KNOW?

All over the world, many people are lactose intolerant. This means their digestive systems can't process the sugar lactose in milk. This genetic condition affects most people of Asian descent.

APPETIZING ATTRACTIONS

➤ "YOGURT LADIES"

On the streets of Seoul, the capital of South Korea, look for a small army of women wearing pink helmets and matching jackets and riding motorized refrigerators—a fridge attached to a motorbike. They deliver yogurt and other dairy products to customers around the city.

➤ KUENDEYLING BAAZAM

At this huge weekend market in Thimphu, Bhutan, you'll have a chance to buy some local datse (soft cheese) and fresh fruits and vegetables from the farmers who grew them.

➤ MAHANE YEHUDA MARKET

In this open-air shuk (marketplace) in Jerusalem, Israel, vendors will sell you a steaming-hot cup of custardy sachlav from a big metal urn. It is made with the ground-up bulbs of the sahlab orchid plant mixed with hot milk, and is often served with shredded coconut.

5 FERMENTED MARE'S MILK
Mongolia

Kumis is a traditional beverage of Mongolia that is made from the fermented milk of a mare, or female horse. It's popular across Central Asia and is often served warm with yak butter mixed in.

ASIA

FOOD FROM THE WATERS

FISHY FOODS

a plate of sushi

From SUSHI to SEAWEED and CAVIAR

With its long coastline and many islands, Asia has lots of seafood. Fish, seaweed, lobster, and other shellfish are popular here. But with more people fishing the waters, governments have had to limit ocean fishing to protect fish stocks. Freshwater fish from rivers and lakes are also part of Asia's wonderful food culture. With such a variety, there's a lot to dive into!

 ## APPETIZING ATTRACTIONS

WATCH A SUSHI CHEF
Sushi is vinegared rice with a little added sugar and salt. It is eaten with raw or cooked fish and vegetables. Whether in Japan—the original home of sushi—or in Hong Kong, Korea, Singapore, Thailand, or elsewhere, sit at a sushi counter and marvel at the chef's skills in wielding sharp knives and creating beautiful and delicious dishes.

TOYOSU MARKET
Tokyo's enormous fish market, opened in 2018 on an artificial island in Tokyo Bay, offers tourists the chance to see live auctions of fresh-caught tuna and other seafood. There are also markets for fresh produce and other food items, restaurants, and viewing areas to take in the sights.

FISH BALL MUSEUM
Fish balls made from fish paste, vegetables, and spices are popular in China and Taiwan. At the Teng Feng Fish Ball Museum in the Xindian District of Taiwan, you can see displays about fishing and manufacturing fish balls—and you might also get the chance to roll your own.

5 COOL FOODS

1 MASGOUF
Iraq

Considered by many to be the Iraqi national dish and said to date back to ancient times, masgouf is a fish—usually carp or barbel—flattened, smoked, and then cooked on the embers of an open fire.

2 YU SHENG
Singapore

In Singapore, the Lunar New Year is celebrated with a raw fish salad and a "prosperity toss." The Cantonese words for "raw fish" and "abundance" both sound like *yu sheng*. So to wish for an abundant new year, diners toss their ingredients into the air with chopsticks. They say the higher the salad goes, the better the coming year will be.

RECORD BREAKER
In 2016, nearly 400 people in Tamana, Japan, helped create the world's longest sushi roll. It was 9,332 feet 8 inches (2,844.61 m) long—about the length of 26 football fields.

3 HILSA FISH CURRY
Bangladesh

Hilsa shad is such an important fish in Bangladesh that the country has declared some of its waters sanctuaries. This effort protects the hilsa population and the livelihood of the fishers who rely on it. Hilsa fish curry, prepared with turmeric, cumin seeds, chilies, and mustard oil, is a popular dish here and among the Bengali people of India.

DIGITAL TRAVELER!
In January 2019, South Korea announced a year-round ban on fishing pollock, a popular fish to eat. Find out what other Asian countries are doing to prevent overfishing of their waters.

Arctic Ocean

EUROPE

RUSSIA

Mediterranean Sea

TURKEY
GEORGIA
ARMENIA
AZERBAIJAN
LEBANON
SYRIA
ISRAEL
JORDAN
IRAQ
TURKMENISTAN
SAUDI ARABIA
KUWAIT
BAHRAIN →
QATAR
UNITED ARAB EMIRATES
YEMEN
OMAN

KAZAKHSTAN

UZBEKISTAN

KYRGYZSTAN
TAJIKISTAN
AFGHANISTAN
PAKISTAN

MONGOLIA

CHINA

NORTH KOREA
SOUTH KOREA
JAPAN

TAIWAN

Pacific Ocean

ASIA

1
4
IRAN

AFRICA

Arabian Sea

INDIA

NEPAL
BHUTAN
BANGLADESH **3**
MYANMAR (BURMA)

Bay of Bengal

SRI LANKA

MALDIVES

5

LAOS
THAILAND
CAMBODIA
VIETNAM

South China Sea

BRUNEI

PHILIPPINES

MALAYSIA **2**
SINGAPORE

Java Sea

INDONESIA

TIMOR-LESTE (EAST TIMOR)

AMOUNT OF FISH CAUGHT
Average pounds (kilograms) per person per year

- More than 132 (60)
- 68–132 (31–60)
- 46–67 (21–30)
- 11–45 (5–20)
- Less than 11 (5)

4 CAVIAR
Iran

Caviar, that famously fancy food, is the cured eggs of some species of sturgeon fish. A lot of caviar comes from Russia, but the rarest and costliest (once sold for more than $15,000 per pound [.45 kg]) is taken from beluga sturgeon kept at a fish farm in the town of Goldasht, Iran.

5 SEAWEED
South Korea

In South Korea, people have eaten seaweed such as kelp for thousands of years. It can be toasted, added to dishes for color and flavoring, or used to wrap rice and other foods, including sushi.

sugary sweets

A SPOONFUL OF SUGAR

ADDING a sprinkle of SWEETNESS

People the world over love to sweeten their food with sugar. The main sources of sucrose—commonly called table sugar—are sugar beets and sugarcane. It's believed that sugar was first cultivated as sugarcane in Southeast Asia. It started spreading around the globe thousands of years ago, carried by boat to islands around the eastern Pacific and Indian Oceans. Honey and many fruits are naturally sweet because they contain various types of sugars. Table sugar can be used in many dishes, but it's most known for sweet treats.

5 COOL FOODS

1 FAIRY BREAD
Australia

It's easy to make this favorite Australian birthday party treat. Just smear butter on white bread and top it off with colored sugar sprinkles.

2 COTTON CANDY
United States

This airy sweet is made of sugar and food coloring. The sugar is heated, liquefied, and spun into tiny strands. Though many countries have some form of this "candy floss," two Americans claim credit for inventing the machine that made the treat a staple at U.S. fairs and carnivals. They introduced it to the public at the 1904 World's Fair, where it was a huge hit.

DIGITAL TRAVELER!
The tallest sugar-cube tower ever built was 6 feet 10 inches (2.08 m) tall. It was made in 2013 in Blanquefort, France, using 2,669 sugar cubes. Grab an adult and look online for photos of other structures built of sugar cubes.

3 PACZKI
Poland

These sugar-coated jelly doughnuts are a favorite in Poland, enjoyed before Lent. Traditionally, people wanted to use up all the sugar and jelly in their cupboards before the Lenten fast started, so they made paczki.

4 SUGARCANE
Vietnam

In Vietnam and other countries where sugarcane is grown, people enjoy the canes as a quick snack. Just peel off the hard outer layer and suck or chew on the inner pulp. Sugarcane juice is also popular.

Map labels:
Arctic Ocean
NORTH AMERICA
EUROPE
ASIA
Pacific Ocean
Atlantic Ocean
AFRICA
Pacific Ocean
SOUTH AMERICA
Indian Ocean
AUSTRALIA
ANTARCTICA

☐ Where sugar beets and sugar cane are grown

5 PASTELITOS
Argentina

On May 25, Argentina's May Revolution Day, people celebrate their country's independence from Spain. They eat pastelitos—little flaky pinwheel-shaped pastry puffs filled with a sweet paste of quince or sweet potato that are deep fried and topped with sugar glaze.

TRUE OR FALSE?

Which of these statements about sugar are true and which are false?

① The world's farms produce more sugarcane than rice.
② Sugar that comes from sugar beets is naturally pink.
③ On average, people in the United States consume about twice as much sugar as people in India.
④ Products from maple trees and bees contain fructose.
⑤ Sweet flavors appeal to dogs ... but not cats.

See answers on page 150.

AFRICA

A RICH VARIETY of MEALS and SNACKS

Africa's landscapes include scorching deserts, snowy mountaintops, and humid jungles. Its people come from hundreds of different groups—including the Amharas of Ethiopia, the Igbo of Nigeria, and the Berbers of North Africa—and speak more than 1,500 different languages. This diversity results in a rich variety of foods served across the continent. People grow dates and olives around the northern oases, and they raise herds of camels, goats, sheep, and cattle on vast grasslands and semi-deserts. They capture wild game on the great savannas. They harvest tropical fruits in the rainforests, and on small farms they grow grains that have been cultivated since ancient times.

Local farmers sell root vegetables at a street market in Freetown, Sierra Leone.

FOODIE HOT SPOTS

 ROASTED SEEDS

Egusi is a melonlike crop grown for its seeds that, in Benin, are used in stews and soups.

 ROOT POWDER

In Ghana, cassava roots are ground into gari, a flour that's used to make porridge.

 GRILLED PLANTAINS

In Cameroon, street vendors sell grilled ripe plantains, which are related to bananas.

 DELICIOUS YAMS

The Igbo people of Nigeria celebrate a yam festival with yam foods and parades.

 GOING TO SEED

People in Guinea use fonio, a nutty-tasting grain, in salads, stews, porridge, and more.

 MADE WITH EGGS

In South Africa, try breyani, a mix of meat, rice, lentils, spices, and hard-boiled eggs.

 CAMEL MILK

The Karrayyu people of Ethiopia are herders who keep camels and drink camel's milk.

 A WELCOME MEAL

Chambo, a fish of Lake Nyasa, is served with corn porridge to welcome guests in Malawi.

 ZESTY SPICES

Many of Africa's diverse cuisines use the bold flavors of indigenous spices such as sesame.

FAST FACTS

Continent size ranking: Second largest
Number of countries: 54
Total population: 1,215,763,000
Largest country by area: Algeria

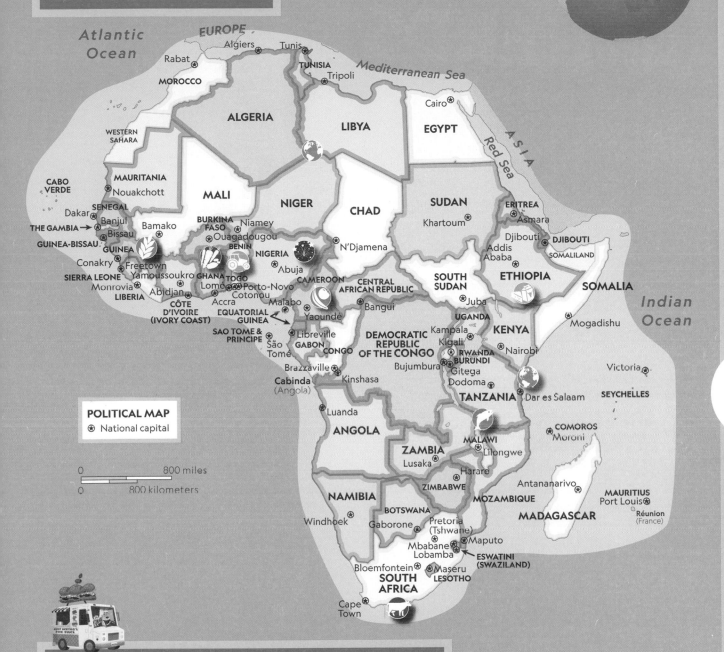

Atlantic Ocean

EUROPE

Mediterranean Sea

ASIA

Red Sea

Indian Ocean

Algiers · Tunis
Rabat
MOROCCO
Tripoli
TUNISIA

WESTERN SAHARA
ALGERIA
LIBYA
EGYPT
Cairo

CABO VERDE
MAURITANIA
Nouakchott
MALI
NIGER
CHAD
SUDAN
Khartoum
ERITREA
Asmara
Djibouti **DJIBOUTI**
SOMALILAND

Dakar
SENEGAL
Banjul
THE GAMBIA →
Bissau
GUINEA-BISSAU
Bamako
BURKINA FASO
Niamey
Ouagadougou
BENIN
N'Djamena
Addis Ababa
ETHIOPIA
SOMALIA

Conakry
GUINEA
Freetown
SIERRA LEONE
Monrovia
LIBERIA
Yamoussoukro
Abidjan
CÔTE D'IVOIRE (IVORY COAST)
GHANA
Lomé **TOGO**
Accra
Porto-Novo
Cotonou
NIGERIA
Abuja
CAMEROON
Malabo
EQUATORIAL GUINEA →
Yaoundé
CENTRAL AFRICAN REPUBLIC
Bangui
SOUTH SUDAN
Juba
UGANDA
Kampala
KENYA
Nairobi
Mogadishu

SAO TOME & PRINCIPE
São Tomé
Libreville
GABON
CONGO
Brazzaville
Kinshasa
DEMOCRATIC REPUBLIC OF THE CONGO
Kigali **RWANDA**
BURUNDI
Bujumbura Gitega
Dodoma
TANZANIA
Dar es Salaam
Victoria
SEYCHELLES

Cabinda (Angola)
Luanda
ANGOLA
ZAMBIA
Lusaka
MALAWI
Lilongwe
COMOROS
Moroni

POLITICAL MAP
⊛ National capital

0 ——— 800 miles
0 ——— 800 kilometers

Windhoek
NAMIBIA
Gaborone
BOTSWANA
Harare
ZIMBABWE
Pretoria (Tshwane)
MOZAMBIQUE
Maputo
Antananarivo
MADAGASCAR
MAURITIUS
Port Louis
Réunion (France)

Mbabane
Lobamba
ESWATINI (SWAZILAND)
Bloemfontein
Maseru
LESOTHO
SOUTH AFRICA
Cape Town

AFRICA

AUNT BERTHA'S FOOD TRAVEL TIPS

* In much of Africa, it's impolite to eat using your left hand, or to use it to touch any serving bowl.

* The same food, or one similar to it, may have different names in different countries in Africa. For example, a thick porridge of cassava, yams, bananas, or grains is called fufu in parts of West Africa, but variations of the dish are called ugali, nshima, and sadza in other places. If you're not sure which word to use, ask!

* Look for food booths or shacks selling tasty treats on street corners, at road intersections, and near bus and train stations. Local specialties vary from place to place.

GARDENS AND HERDS

plowing the land using oxen in Ethiopia

From DATES and GRAINS to TROPICAL FRUITS

People were raising plants and animals for food in Africa more than 5,000 years ago. The ancient Egyptians, for example, grew grains, vegetables, and fruits along the Nile River. Modern African farmers generally raise a garden and a few animals. To feed the continent's growing population, individual governments and international organizations are teaching people how to grow more food on their land.

APPETIZING ATTRACTIONS

DESERT FARM
Look for rows of leafy green olive trees at the Wadi Food farm, outside Cairo, Egypt. When planting olives in the hot, dry Egyptian desert, farmers sometimes plant palm trees, too—to shade the olive trees and cool the air.

FARM SANCTUARY
At Sanctuary Farm at Lake Naivasha, Kenya, see impalas, wildebeests, zebras, and giraffes grazing alongside dairy cows. Farm owners milk their cows while also conserving their lands to protect wildlife.

SPICE UP YOUR DAY
On the island of Zanzibar off Tanzania's coast, tour a spice farm to see vanilla orchids, cinnamon, coffee, cayenne pepper, clove, and other fragrant plants—and maybe take a taste.

RECORD BREAKER
The African Rhino Horn banana plant can grow fruits up to two feet (61 cm) long! It's become popular among gardeners as an ornamental plant, and those supersize bananas are handy if you're really hungry.

5 COOL FOODS

1 GARDEN EGG
Uganda

Called the garden egg because of its small size and egglike shape, this crunchy fruit grows in gardens throughout Africa south of the Sahara. It comes in a variety of colors—white, red, lime green, pink, black, and even striped. Most garden eggs taste slightly bitter, but they can be eaten raw, or boiled, steamed, pickled, or added to meat and vegetable stews. The fruit is actually an eggplant, though it looks more like a tomato.

2 HUMPED CATTLE
South Sudan

What's that cow with the hump on its back? It's a zebu! Zebu cattle are well adapted to tropical countries. They were originally from Asia, and people brought them to Africa thousands of years ago. You'll recognize a zebu by the big fatty hump over its shoulders. Many zebu cattle also have a long fold of skin—called a dewlap—under their neck. Farmers in South Sudan raise zebus for their milk.

3 MONKEY BREAD
Niger

The baobab tree grows wild in low-lying areas across Africa. In Niger, people also cultivate this valuable tree. The leaves, flowers, and roots are edible, and the fruit, sometimes called monkey bread, is used to make flour, porridge, and drinks. The name may have come from the fact that monkeys enjoy eating the fruit or that its pulp resembles bread.

4 AMARANTH
Tanzania

This leafy green vegetable grows well in East Africa's moist areas. People use the leaves for stir-fries or add them raw to salads. Some amaranth species are grown for their seeds. Boil up the amaranth seeds for a nice hot porridge for breakfast.

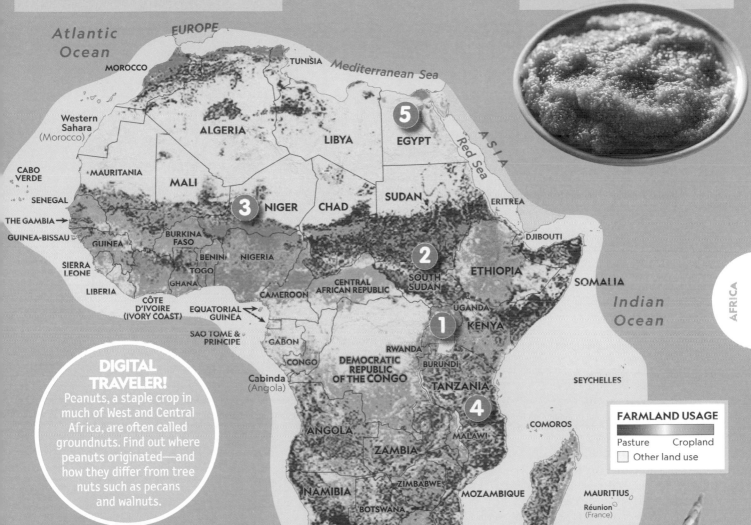

Atlantic Ocean

EUROPE

MOROCCO

TUNISIA

Mediterranean Sea

Western Sahara (Morocco)

ALGERIA

LIBYA

EGYPT

5

Red Sea

ASIA

CABO VERDE

MAURITANIA

MALI

NIGER

CHAD

SUDAN

ERITREA

SENEGAL

THE GAMBIA →

GUINEA-BISSAU

GUINEA

BURKINA FASO

BENIN

NIGERIA

DJIBOUTI

3

SIERRA LEONE

LIBERIA

TOGO

GHANA

CÔTE D'IVOIRE (IVORY COAST)

CAMEROON

CENTRAL AFRICAN REPUBLIC

SOUTH SUDAN

2

ETHIOPIA

SOMALIA

Indian Ocean

EQUATORIAL GUINEA →

SAO TOME & PRINCIPE

GABON

CONGO

DEMOCRATIC REPUBLIC OF THE CONGO

UGANDA

KENYA

1

AFRICA

Cabinda (Angola)

RWANDA

BURUNDI

TANZANIA

4

SEYCHELLES

ANGOLA

ZAMBIA

MALAWI

COMOROS

NAMIBIA

ZIMBABWE

BOTSWANA

MOZAMBIQUE

MADAGASCAR

MAURITIUS

Réunion (France)

ESWATINI (SWAZILAND)

SOUTH AFRICA

LESOTHO

FARMLAND USAGE

Pasture — Cropland

☐ Other land use

DIGITAL TRAVELER!
Peanuts, a staple crop in much of West and Central Africa, are often called groundnuts. Find out where peanuts originated—and how they differ from tree nuts such as pecans and walnuts.

5 SORGHUM
Egypt

This grain, cultivated across Africa, can be cooked like rice or popped like popcorn. It needs less water than wheat or corn. Sorghum is used in cooked dishes, salads, and snacks. Ground into flour, it is used to make pies, cookies, and bread.

MIGHTY ROOTS

vegetables for sale at a farmers market in Tanzania

From YAMS and CASSAVA to SPICY BARK

The huge variety of African plants means there are lots of local vegetables with different textures, tastes, and smells to choose from. In many countries, root crops are important staples—especially sweet potatoes, yams, and cassava (also called manioc). The leaves of bananas and other plants are handy for wrapping and cooking. In many places in Africa, people grow greens and other vegetables in small gardens. And plants growing in the wild add even more variety to African meals.

DIGITAL TRAVELER!
Indigenous African vegetables such as celosia, enset, and moringa have been largely replaced by imported crops like rice. Grab an adult and search online to find out how they are still used in meals today.

5 COOL FOODS

1 MATAPA
Mozambique

Cassava leaves are tasty when cooked in garlic, onion, coconut, and peanut sauce to make matapa. Similar cooked-greens dishes, such as ifisashi in Malawi and Zambia, and sukuma wiki in Kenya, use different greens and seasonings.

DID YOU KNOW?
The hibiscus flower looks pretty, and tastes pretty good, too—it's tart, like cranberries. People in Senegal use hibiscus to create a cool drink called bissap, which is sometimes frozen into a Popsicle-like treat. Added flavorings may include honey, ginger, or pepper. Yum!

2 IRIO
Kenya

A favorite Kenyan comfort food, irio is made of potatoes, peas, beans, corn, and onion mashed together. Try it with spiced, roasted meat for a delicious meal.

EUROPE
MOROCCO
Western Sahara (Morocco)
ALGERIA
CABO VERDE
MAURITANIA
MALI
SENEGAL
THE GAMBIA →
GUINEA-BISSAU
GUINEA
BURKINA FASO
BENIN
SIERRA LEONE
TOGO
GHANA
LIBERIA
CÔTE D'IVOIRE (IVORY COAST)
3
Atlantic Ocean

3 FUFU
Ghana

This sticky, starchy dish, sometimes called foufou or foutou, is made from root crops like yam or cassava that are pounded or grated into a solid mash. It's a food staple in West African countries. In Ghana, which claims to have invented it, fufu is made with unripe plantain and boiled cassava pounded together with a large stick. To eat it, grab a portion (with your right hand), form a ball, dip it in a flavorful soup or sauce, and enjoy.

4 LIGUSHA
Eswatini

Ligusha is a plant that grows wild in much of Africa. In Eswatini, the leaves are boiled and served as a soupy dish. Ligusha is also popular in Egypt, where it's often served with fish or rice. This plant goes by different local names, including wild jute, delele, and thelele.

5 CINNAMON
Tanzania

This favorite spice comes from the bark of cinnamon trees. Cinnamon trees—which are native to Sri Lanka—are cultivated on Zanzibar spice farms, off the coast of Tanzania. The spice is used in desserts, pastries, salads, and breakfast cereals. It has such a strong aroma, you can smell it in the air around the trees.

AFRICA

ROOTS and TUBERS PRODUCTION*
U.S. tons per acre
(metric tons per hectare)

- More than 5.7 (12.7)
- 5.7 (12.7) or less
- 0

*Not all roots and tubers shown

APPETIZING ATTRACTIONS

MOUNTAIN MARKET
When in Morocco, have a snack and a drink at a souk, or public market. Souk el Tieta, located in a small village near the Atlas Mountains, is held on Tuesday evenings and features acrobats, storytellers, musicians, and beautiful crafts, along with piles of spices and local fruits and vegetables.

RIDE AROUND A FARM
In the countryside of Limuru, Kenya, tour Kawamwaki Farm—on horseback. This farm produces fresh vegetables for the city and offers tourists the chance to enjoy a horseback ride around its fields. You can also pick up a basket of organic veggies, fresh eggs, or milk.

SAMPLE SUGARCANE
Visit the Sugarcane Museum in Tambankulu, Eswatini, where you can tour a sugarcane field and crush sugarcane. Then sample some freshly crushed sugarcane juice at the museum café.

95

5 COOL FOODS

1 BUNNY CHOW
South Africa

This popular street food in the city of Durban is a spicy curry served in a half loaf of white bread. Immigrants to South Africa from India adapted recipes from their home country, using local ingredients. Originally a bean dish, bunny chow today is often made with meat (no rabbit, though) and vegetables.

2 MATOKE
Uganda

The matoke is a short, thick banana indigenous to southwest Uganda. Matoke is also the name of a Ugandan dish. While green, the fruits are peeled, steamed, and mashed or cut into pieces. Then they are added to vegetables and meat, such as beef or goat, to make a stew.

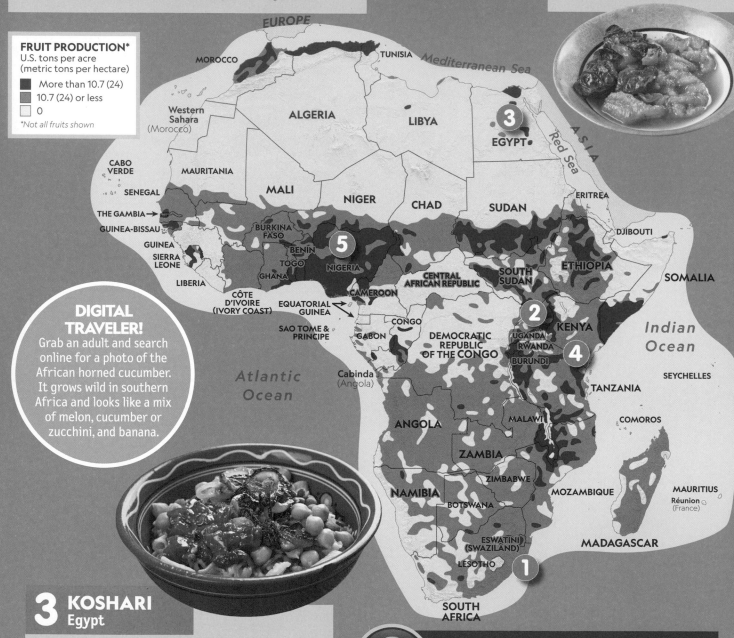

FRUIT PRODUCTION*
U.S. tons per acre
(metric tons per hectare)

- More than 10.7 (24)
- 10.7 (24) or less
- 0

*Not all fruits shown

EUROPE

MOROCCO · TUNISIA · *Mediterranean Sea* · ASIA

Western Sahara (Morocco) · ALGERIA · LIBYA · EGYPT · ③ · *Red Sea*

CABO VERDE · MAURITANIA · MALI · NIGER · CHAD · SUDAN · ERITREA · DJIBOUTI

SENEGAL · THE GAMBIA → · GUINEA-BISSAU · GUINEA · BURKINA FASO · BENIN · TOGO · NIGERIA · ⑤ · CENTRAL AFRICAN REPUBLIC · SOUTH SUDAN · ETHIOPIA · SOMALIA

SIERRA LEONE · GHANA · LIBERIA · CÔTE D'IVOIRE (IVORY COAST) · EQUATORIAL GUINEA → · CAMEROON

SAO TOME & PRINCIPE · GABON · CONGO · DEMOCRATIC REPUBLIC OF THE CONGO · UGANDA · ② · KENYA · RWANDA · BURUNDI · ④ · *Indian Ocean*

Cabinda (Angola) · SEYCHELLES · TANZANIA · COMOROS

Atlantic Ocean

ANGOLA · ZAMBIA · MALAWI · ZIMBABWE · MOZAMBIQUE · MAURITIUS · Réunion (France)

NAMIBIA · BOTSWANA · ESWATINI (SWAZILAND) · MADAGASCAR

LESOTHO · ① · SOUTH AFRICA

DIGITAL TRAVELER!
Grab an adult and search online for a photo of the African horned cucumber. It grows wild in southern Africa and looks like a mix of melon, cucumber or zucchini, and banana.

3 KOSHARI
Egypt

This dish, also called koushari or koshary, is an Egyptian specialty made with rice, lentils, macaroni, garlic, chickpeas, and spicy tomato sauce, and topped with fried onion. Street vendors, or "koshari men," serve it from carts, scooping up each ingredient into a bowl for hungry customers.

STRANGE BUT TRUE
A native West African fruit known as *Synsepalum dulcificum* is also called "miracle berry" or "miracle fruit." Why? Eating it alters your taste buds. For an hour or so after you eat these berries, other foods will taste sweet—even lemons.

caption: fresh okra

PLENTIFUL PRODUCE

MANGOES, okra, peanuts, and PEAS

With many different habitats and climates, Africa has a rich mix of fruits and legumes, from tropical mangoes to peanuts and peas. Many of these food plants grow wild, while others are raised on farms and orchards. Whether they're handpicked in the wild or harvested by machine, Africa's fruits, nuts, and legumes lend their characteristic flavors and textures to local meals. People from different backgrounds, both indigenous and immigrant, bring their traditions to the table, producing a range of tasty dishes that are served at street stalls and in cafés.

AFRICA

4 KACHUMBARI
Kenya

In much of East Africa, people enjoy this tasty side dish. It's a fresh onion and tomato salad, often made with avocado, that is served cold with meat or fish.

APPETIZING ATTRACTIONS

CHOCOLATE FOREST

In the tiny, two-island nation of Sao Tome and Principe, look for cacao plantations spread across green hillsides. Claudio Corallo's chocolate factory in Sao Tome uses its cacao beans to make intense, rich chocolate. Stop by the factory for a tour—and make sure to stay for the chocolate tasting!

ORGANIC GARDENS

At Gibb's Farm in Karatu, Tanzania, explore organic fruit and vegetable gardens, help the staff with harvesting, and try milking a cow. After that, enjoy a meal made from fresh garden produce.

DATES IN THE DESERT

In Tunisia, natural oases filled with date palms are scattered across the southern desert. At the oasis town of Tozeur, visit the Eden Palm museum and farm to see date farmers in action and sample delicious dates.

5 OKRA
Nigeria

Okra plants, native to Africa, are grown for their seed pods, sometimes called "lady's fingers." In Nigeria, these mild, somewhat slimy green pods are used to make a spicy soup that also contains palm oil, pumpkin leaves, and meat, fish, or crayfish. Okra soup is called *miyan kubewa* in the Hausa language and *obe ila* in Yoruba.

TIME TO CELEBRATE

celebrating the Muslim festival of Tabaski

Appetizing EVENTS and HOLIDAYS

Africa has a mouthwatering assortment of foods and plenty of festivals to celebrate them. Across the continent, you'll see religious holidays and traditional customs that are observed with special meals and celebrations where tourists are invited to taste local delicacies. Find such a gathering and tuck into some local cultural specialties!

5 COOL FOOD EVENTS

1. Uganda
2. Nigeria
3. Morocco
4. Algeria
5. Senegal

1 ROLEX FESTIVAL
Uganda

This August festival in Kampala doesn't celebrate wristwatches. It's held in honor of a favorite food. The rolex is a rolled snack in which a thin egg omelet is rolled up with vegetables in a flatbread called chapati. Chapati, which originated in India, is popular throughout East Africa.

2 FISHING FESTIVAL
Nigeria

Each spring in Argungu, northern Nigeria, crowds gather by the Matan Fada River for a four-day festival. The event, which features Nigerian music and dance, marks the end of the crop-growing season and harvest and celebrates the importance of fish as a food for the local communities. One highlight is the fishing contest. Locals swarm into the water and catch fish using traditional nets and gourds. The person who catches the largest fish wins a prize.

3 EID AL-FITR
Morocco

The Muslim holy month of Ramadan comes in the ninth month of the Islamic calendar. In that month, adult Muslims fast during the daytime. Ramadan ends with Eid al-Fitr, a three-day feast. In the city of Fez, Eid is often kicked off with street events before families settle down for the first daytime meal in a month. At this time, street vendors traditionally make and sell samosas and sweet candy snacks.

4 COUSCOUS FESTIVAL
Algeria

Not all traditions are old. The International Couscous Festival, held in Algiers, Algeria, was first celebrated in February 2018. Chefs gathered from many countries to create dishes using couscous, an important food across northern Africa. Couscous, made of tiny pastalike balls of durum wheat, is mixed with vegetables, meats, and spices.

TRY THIS RECIPE

ROLEX SANDWICH
A TASTE OF UGANDA

This "roll of eggs" snack can be modified by adding thin slices of mushrooms and peppers.

Prep time: 15 minutes
Serving: 1 person

1 small tomato
1 egg
salt to taste
2 tablespoons vegetable oil
1 large (9-inch) ready-made chapati (Indian flatbread) or flour tortilla
⅓ cup shredded cabbage (any kind)

1. Cut three thin slices of tomato. Cut each slice in half. Set aside.
2. Break the egg into a small cup. Add a pinch of salt and beat with a fork.
3. With an adult's help, heat the vegetable oil over medium heat in a large nonstick pan.
4. Pour the egg into the pan. Cook one side for 1–2 minutes until slightly brown. Flip the egg using a heat-proof spatula. Cook the other side.
5. Lift the cooked egg with the spatula and slide the chapati underneath. Heat for 20 seconds.
6. Move the egg-covered chapati to a plate.
7. Place the cabbage and add tomato slices in a strip on the right side of the chapati. Add salt to taste.
8. With an adult's help, when the chapati is cool enough to touch, start at the right edge and fold the chapati over the strip of filling. Continue rolling up the chapati and egg until you have made a complete wrap. Serve hot.

AFRICA

5 TABASKI
Senegal

Muslims around the world celebrate Eid al-Adha, the Feast of Sacrifice, in the last month of the Islamic calendar. In Senegal and elsewhere in West Africa, this holiday is known as Tabaski. Many families sacrifice a sheep or ram for the main meal at home of this important holiday. Local food stalls and cafés serve lamb dishes.

99

CORN SNACK

In the market mazes of Dar es Salaam, Tanzania, and other cities of East Africa, roasted corn on the cob is a favorite food. You might find it spiced up with ginger or other seasonings.

DRIVE-BY DOUGHNUTS

Puff puffs, Sierra Leone's deep-fried dough balls, are a version of doughnuts. In Freetown, look for street vendors selling them by the roadside. These little bites go by other names in other countries—such as bofrot in Ghana.

PLENTIFUL PLAINS

Africa's grasslands, or savannas, are home to a variety of animals, from huge elephants to tiny termites. If you visit, keep an eye out for the vast array of plants, too. Edible grains like sorghum and millet, and tasty fruits including figs and plums grow here.

DIGITAL TRAVELER!

Mageu, a popular drink in South Africa, is made with corn. Find out how it's made and why it's a popular thirst quencher.

millet grains

5 COOL FOODS

1 MALVA PUDDING
South Africa

Malva pudding, or *malvapoeding* in the Afrikaans language, is a sweet dessert served in many South African restaurants. This spongy cake, made with wheat or corn flour, is sweetened with apricot jam and covered with a rich sweet cream sauce. The original recipe came from Dutch settlers about 300 years ago.

GREAT GRAINS

CEREAL CHOICES

Porridge, PASTRIES, PIES, and puff puffs

P eople have gathered Africa's wild grasses and cooked their seeds, or cereal grains, for thousands of years. Some cereals indigenous to Africa, including sorghum and millet, are major crops today.

Wheat, corn, and rice have also been imported to this continent and are grown on the plains as crops. Corn is now a staple in much of Africa. Rice is widely eaten in West Africa. Many grains—such as millet, sorghum, and corn—are used to make porridge or are ground to make flour for baking and making sweet desserts.

2 COUSCOUS
Algeria

Couscous is neither a grain nor pasta, but rather steamed tiny balls of wheat flour. A popular Algerian meal is couscous served with chunks of meat, olives, and vegetables, seasoned with black pepper, cumin, and other spices.

GRAIN PRODUCTION*

U.S. tons per acre
(metric tons per hectare)

- ▮ More than 0.1 (0.3)
- ▮ 0.1 (0.3) or less
- ▯ 0

*Not all grains shown

ASIA

Mediterranean Sea

Red Sea

EUROPE

Indian Ocean

Atlantic Ocean

TUNISIA
MOROCCO
Western Sahara (Morocco)
ALGERIA
LIBYA
EGYPT
MAURITANIA
MALI
NIGER
CHAD
SUDAN
ERITREA
DJIBOUTI
ETHIOPIA
SOMALIA
CABO VERDE
SENEGAL
THE GAMBIA
GUINEA-BISSAU
GUINEA
SIERRA LEONE
LIBERIA
CÔTE D'IVOIRE (IVORY COAST)
BURKINA FASO
GHANA
TOGO
BENIN
NIGERIA
CAMEROON
EQUATORIAL GUINEA
SAO TOME & PRINCIPE
GABON
CONGO
Cabinda (Angola)
CENTRAL AFRICAN REPUBLIC
SOUTH SUDAN
UGANDA
KENYA
RWANDA
BURUNDI
DEMOCRATIC REPUBLIC OF THE CONGO
TANZANIA
ANGOLA
ZAMBIA
MALAWI
MOZAMBIQUE
ZIMBABWE
NAMIBIA
BOTSWANA
ESWATINI (SWAZILAND)
LESOTHO
SOUTH AFRICA
MADAGASCAR
COMOROS
MAURITIUS
Réunion (France)
SEYCHELLES

3 JOLLOF
Nigeria

This simple, spicy, one-pot dish is a mixture of rice, tomatoes, onions, and peppers. Often, meat or fish is added, too. Cafés and stalls in Nigeria and elsewhere in West Africa serve jollof on its own or with soup and fried vegetables.

4 INJERA
Eritrea

This spongy flatbread is eaten with stews and other dishes. Often it is used to scoop up the food, or it may even be used as the tray on which the food is served. It's made from teff, an ancient grain grown in Eritrea and Ethiopia.

5 B'STILLA
Morocco

In Marrakech, look for vendors selling this tasty meat pie. It has folded layers of paper-thin pastry made from wheat flour, and it's stuffed with shredded pigeon or chicken meat and a nutty, spicy filling.

DID YOU KNOW?

Ethiopia is home to some of the world's fastest long-distance runners. What's their secret? Perhaps it's the teff in their diets? Teff is a grain that has been grown and eaten in Ethiopia for thousands of years. Its mineral and protein content are very nutritious.

TRADITIONAL DISHES

strips of biltong

SPICY BLENDS and slow-cooked STEWS

The meat served in Africa comes from many different sources. People eat chickens raised in farmers' yards and meat from cattle, camels, and goats tended by nomadic herders. In some areas, traditional foods may include wild antelope or specially prepared caterpillars. In various places across the continent, many meat dishes are served in different ways, allowing diners to enjoy a wide range of regional flavors. As you travel, search for local ingredients, dishes, and cooking methods, and try some of the distinctive meat and poultry dishes offered along the way.

5 COOL FOODS

1 PERI PERI CHICKEN
Mozambique

This favorite food of Mozambique—grilled chicken with plenty of hot, spicy seasonings like chili pepper, cilantro, ginger, and garlic—may have come from Portugal. It is usually served with a mix of cooked local vegetables.

2 SHAKSHUKA
Tunisia

Poached eggs top off a skillet full of simmering tomatoes and peppers in this Tunisian dish. Shakshuka, sometimes called ojja or jazz-mazz, can be baked in the oven or cooked on top of the stove. The name shakshuka comes from the Arabic word for "mix."

3 POULET YASSA
Senegal

This chicken dish is for onion lovers! Before cooking, the meat is soaked in a marinade of onions and lemons. Then it is grilled and topped with an onion and lemon sauce so the meat is tender, full of flavor, and delicious. Poulet yassa is usually served with rice and olives.

RECORD BREAKER

In 2017, a group of people in Cabo Verde cooked huge amounts of chicken, pork, corn, beans, and vegetables in an enormous vat to make the world's largest batch of cachupa stew, a traditional local dish. More than 30,000 people helped eat the gigantic dish.

Atlantic Ocean

EUROPE

MOROCCO

TUNISIA ② *Mediterranean Sea*

Western Sahara (Morocco)

ALGERIA

LIBYA

EGYPT

Red Sea

CABO VERDE

MAURITANIA

MALI

NIGER

CHAD

SUDAN

ERITREA

SENEGAL ③

THE GAMBIA →

GUINEA-BISSAU

GUINEA

SIERRA LEONE

LIBERIA

BURKINA FASO

BENIN

NIGERIA

TOGO

GHANA

CÔTE D'IVOIRE (IVORY COAST)

EQUATORIAL GUINEA →

SÃO TOMÉ & PRÍNCIPE

GABON

CONGO

CAMEROON

CENTRAL AFRICAN REPUBLIC

DEMOCRATIC REPUBLIC OF THE CONGO

UGANDA

SOUTH SUDAN

ETHIOPIA

SOMALIA

DJIBOUTI

KENYA

RWANDA

BURUNDI

Cabinda (Angola)

TANZANIA

ANGOLA

ZAMBIA

MALAWI

COMOROS

Indian Ocean

NAMIBIA

BOTSWANA

ZIMBABWE ⑤

MOZAMBIQUE

MAURITIUS

Réunion (France)

①

④

ESWATINI (SWAZILAND)

MADAGASCAR

SOUTH AFRICA

LESOTHO

AFRICA

DIGITAL TRAVELER!
Antelope, including springbok, impalas, and kudus, roam wild in Africa. Some people eat their meat. Find some African recipes using antelope or other game meat.

CATTLE PRODUCTION
Number per square mile
(number per square kilometer)
- More than 129 (50)
- 129 (50) or less
- 0

4 POTJIEKOS
South Africa

This Afrikaans word means "pot food," because this dish is cooked outdoors in a heavy three-legged pot. The pot is filled with a layer of meat (often lamb), a layer of vegetables, then a layer of pasta, rice, potato, or another starchy food. It's then heated slowly for several hours. Potjiekos is very popular in Johannesburg.

5 MOPANE WORMS
Botswana

This nutritious delicacy isn't really worms, but rather the caterpillars of the emperor moth. The wormlike critters are usually found on mopane trees, and people consider them to be delicious. They can be eaten raw, dried, or cooked with tomatoes, garlic, peanuts, and chilies and served as a crispy snack or in a tasty stew.

APPETIZING ATTRACTIONS

➦ STREET FOOD ON A STICK
Look for vendors selling bits of chicken and other meats on skewers—marinated and roasted outside on a grill. This street food is called suya in Nigeria and chichinga in Ghana.

➦ BILTONG FROM THE BUTCHER
Biltong is a jerky-like South African speciality made with raw meat that is cut into pieces and hung up to dry. You can buy it from local butchers. In Johannesburg, order your biltong as you like it: ostrich or beef, fatty or lean, plain or very spicy.

➦ BUSTLING MARKET
In Ouagadougou, the capital of Burkina Faso, don't miss the Central Market. Just follow the noise! This large market is crammed with sounds and activity, as people shout to sell their wares. You might even see farmers selling live chickens.

DIVERSE DAIRY

selling cheese in Egypt

Cheese and CURDS from cattle and CAMELS

People in Africa drink less milk, on average, than those on other continents, but dairy consumption is on the rise. Many groups, such as the nomadic Maasai in Kenya and the rural Bodi tribe in Ethiopia, have a long tradition of keeping small dairy herds. In Kenya, there are about 600,000 small herds of dairy cows—most with only about five cows. In many areas, Africans raise small numbers of sheep or goats for their milk. And in the deserts of North Africa, herders keep camels, which are well adapted to the harsh conditions and produce plenty of milk for people to drink and quench that desert thirst.

5 COOL FOODS

1 MELKTERT
South Africa

A melktert—milk tart—is a spiced custard pie that's a South African favorite for birthday parties, afternoon tea, school bake sales, and after-dinner dessert. Dutch dairy farmers brought this recipe to Cape Town, South Africa, in the 1600s. It's made with milk, sugar, eggs, and cinnamon.

2 GOAT'S MILK CHEESE
Morocco

Goats thrive in locations where there's not enough pasture to keep cows, because goats don't eat as much grass as cows do. The nomadic Tuareg people of the Sahara keep goats and use their milk to make toma, a traditional cheese you can buy in stores and from street vendors. Goat's milk, butter, and other goat cheeses made from it are available, too.

3 "CAMELBERT" CHEESE
Mauritania

Nomadic herders in northern Africa traditionally get milk from the camels they keep. Cheesemakers in Mauritania buy camel milk from local herders to make cheeses. One type of cheese they make has been nicknamed "camelbert" because it is similar to soft French camembert cheese.

4 ZA'ATAR YOGURT
Tunisia

Cool yogurt blends well with hot and spicy flavors. In this Tunisian combination, roasted beets are mixed with yogurt, chickpeas, za'atar—a blend of thyme, sumac, and sesame seeds— and harissa—a hot chili pepper paste.

5 BABUTE
Congo

For a dish that is wholesome and filling, try babute—essentially a combination of milk, cream, eggs, minced beef, apricots, and a little curry powder. The recipe can vary depending on what ingredients—often leftovers—are available or what a cook wants to use.

DIGITAL TRAVELER!
What is Bombay Crush? Bombay is the former name of Mumbai, India. Find out why this South African treat got its name from an Indian city.

EUROPE

TUNISIA 4

Mediterranean Sea

MOROCCO 2

Western Sahara (Morocco)

3

ALGERIA

LIBYA

EGYPT

A S I A

Red Sea

CABO VERDE

MAURITANIA

MALI

NIGER

CHAD

SUDAN

ERITREA

SENEGAL

THE GAMBIA →

GUINEA-BISSAU

GUINEA

SIERRA LEONE

BURKINA FASO

BENIN

NIGERIA

TOGO

GHANA

DJIBOUTI

ETHIOPIA

SOMALIA

SOUTH SUDAN

CENTRAL AFRICAN REPUBLIC

Atlantic Ocean

LIBERIA

CÔTE D'IVOIRE (IVORY COAST)

EQUATORIAL GUINEA →

SAO TOME & PRINCIPE

CAMEROON

GABON

CONGO

5

DEMOCRATIC REPUBLIC OF THE CONGO

UGANDA

RWANDA

BURUNDI

KENYA

TANZANIA

Indian Ocean

SEYCHELLES

Cabinda (Angola)

AFRICA

ANGOLA

ZAMBIA

MALAWI

COMOROS

ZIMBABWE

MOZAMBIQUE

MADAGASCAR

NAMIBIA

BOTSWANA

ESWATINI (SWAZILAND)

SOUTH AFRICA

LESOTHO

1

MILK PRODUCTION
U.S. tons per acre (metric tons per hectare)
- More than 0.1 (0.2)
- 0.02–0.1 (0.05–0.2)
- 0.01–0.02 (0.03–0.05)
- 0.004–0.009 (0.01–0.02)
- Less than 0.004 (0.01)
- No data

APPETIZING ATTRACTIONS

⤷ CHEESE FARM AND FACTORY
Brown's Cheese dairy farm outside Nairobi, Kenya, lets you tour its farm and cheese factory, watch cows being milked, taste farm-made cheese, and stay for a three-course lunch, which might include pizza and ice cream.

⤷ ICE CREAM ON BIKES
In South Africa, look for people on bicycles selling ice cream. The bikes have been fitted with a special cooler to keep the frozen sweet treats nice and cold.

⤷ GOATS APLENTY
If you're in Gambia, visit the Gambia Goat Dairy in Sanyang Village to see a new project bringing commercial goat milking to this small nation. Its founders hope to help provide food and milk for the growing population.

? DID YOU KNOW?
The Maasai people of Kenya and Tanzania don't often eat beef, but they do drink cow's milk and sometimes cow's blood. They carefully take the blood from the neck of a live cow, leaving no lasting damage to the animal.

TASTY CATCHES

Nile perch

PERCH, sardines, lobsters, and SHRIMPS

People in Africa have long relied on fish for food. Bodies of water, including the Nile and Congo Rivers, Lake Victoria, the Mediterranean Sea, and the Indian and Atlantic Oceans, provide a bounty of fish and other foods. The harvest from these waters is flavored with local ingredients and prepared according to local tastes and traditions. In recent years, many of the waters in and around Africa have been overfished. Governments and concerned organizations have introduced aquaculture, or fish farming, to regulate this and take pressure off the dwindling fish populations in the wild.

RECORD BREAKER

People living along the Nile River eat Nile perch, Africa's largest freshwater fish. The largest Nile perch ever caught with a fishing rod and reel (with a photo taken) weighed 249 pounds (113 kg) and measured 82 inches (2.1 m) long.

5 COOL FOODS

APPETIZING ATTRACTIONS

FISHERS AT WORK
At fishing villages on the Seychelles islands in the Indian Ocean, look for colorfully painted wooden fishing boats and local fishers using traditional hand lines, nets, and basket traps to make their catch. Small cafés and street stalls offer a variety of fish dishes made with each day's catch.

GREAT AFRICAN LAKE
Lake Victoria, the world's largest tropical lake, sits at the border of Tanzania, Uganda, and Kenya. More than 200 fish species live in the lake. Visit a fishing village, such as Ggaba in Kampala, Uganda, to sample some of the local catch.

GROWING FISH
The Makindi Fish Farm near Thika in Kenya raises catfish and tilapia in more than 90 ponds. You can visit the farm to see the hatchery, ponds, and packing plant.

1 FISH CALULU
Angola

Fish calulu, or calulu de peixe, is a traditional Angolan dish made with fresh, smoked, or dried fish, palm oil, spices, and vegetables such as okra, onion, tomato, and sweet potato leaves or spinach. Calulu is made with one of many fish and is usually served with funje, a cassava porridge.

2 KAPENTA
Zambia

The kapenta, or Tanganyika sardine, is a small freshwater fish native to Lake Tanganyika. Often sold by street vendors, kapenta can be dried in the sun, or cooked fresh and eaten with corn porridge.

3 KARIBA TILAPIA
Zimbabwe

Tilapia, including a species known locally as Kariba tilapia, are one of the many different types of native fish found in Lake Kariba, which is located on the border of Zimbabwe and Zambia. Due to the threat of invasive species, fish farms in Zimbabwe are producing sustainably farm-raised tilapia. Try a crispy whole fish with a side salad.

DIGITAL TRAVELER!
Grab an adult and go online to find out why certain catfish found in Africa's Lake Chad are known as "upside-down" species.

AMOUNT OF FISH CAUGHT
Average pounds (kilograms) per person per year

- More than 132 (60)
- 68–132 (31–60)
- 46–67 (21–30)
- 11–45 (5–20)
- Less than 11 (5)

EUROPE

MOROCCO
Western Sahara (Morocco)
ALGERIA
TUNISIA
Mediterranean Sea
LIBYA
EGYPT
ASIA
Red Sea

CABO VERDE
MAURITANIA
MALI
NIGER
CHAD
SUDAN
ERITREA
DJIBOUTI
SENEGAL
THE GAMBIA →
GUINEA-BISSAU
GUINEA
SIERRA LEONE
LIBERIA
BURKINA FASO
BENIN
TOGO
GHANA
NIGERIA
CÔTE D'IVOIRE (IVORY COAST)
EQUATORIAL GUINEA →
SAO TOME & PRINCIPE
CAMEROON
CENTRAL AFRICAN REPUBLIC
SOUTH SUDAN
ETHIOPIA
SOMALIA

Atlantic Ocean

GABON
CONGO
DEMOCRATIC REPUBLIC OF THE CONGO
Cabinda (Angola)
UGANDA
RWANDA
BURUNDI
KENYA
TANZANIA
Indian Ocean
SEYCHELLES
COMOROS

AFRICA

4 LANGOUSTE À LA VANILLE
Comoros

The East African country of Comoros is a group of islands in the Indian Ocean east of Mozambique. The food here is influenced by French and Middle Eastern cultures, and by the rich resources of the sea. A favorite dish is langouste à la vanille—locally caught lobster with vanilla cream sauce.

ANGOLA
ZAMBIA
MALAWI
ZIMBABWE
MOZAMBIQUE
MADAGASCAR
Réunion (France)
MAURITIUS
NAMIBIA
BOTSWANA
ESWATINI (SWAZILAND)
SOUTH AFRICA
LESOTHO

5 SPICY PRAWNS
Mozambique

With its long Indian Ocean coastline, Mozambique offers a menu with plenty of seafood. A popular meal is shrimps or prawns with spicy peri peri sauce—hot peppers, paprika, garlic, and lime. It's often eaten with bread to soak up the tasty sauce!

ZESTY SPICES

SPECTACULAR flavors and SEASONINGS

For thousands of years, people in Africa and around the world have used spices and herbs to flavor their food and to cure various aches and pains. Long ago, certain spices were costly and in great demand because they were rare and grew only in limited tropical regions. Traders brought spices such as cinnamon and cassia from Asia and Oceania into the Middle East about 4,000 years ago. The spice trade spread from there to Europe. But the traders refused to say where they got the spices, so European explorers began expeditions to seek new routes to the lands where spices grew. Eventually, these travels resulted in the colonization of new lands. Today, spices and herbs are farmed and sold all over the world. Each region's traditional spices still give the local cuisine its characteristic flavors.

an array of spices

TRUE OR FALSE?

Which of these statements about herbs and spices are true and which are false?

1. Bay leaves, from from the bay laurel tree, taste different depending on whether they're grown in California or Turkey.

2. The United States is the world's largest importer of spices.

3. Herbs and spices both come from a plant's leaves.

4. Paprika is the national spice of Guatemala.

5. On a scale measuring the spiciness of peppers, a green bell pepper scores 0 while the superhot Carolina Reaper scores up to 2,200,000 heat units.

See answers on page 150.

5 COOL FOODS

2 CARAWAY
Germany

Caraway seeds are among the few spices native to Europe. The seeds are often used in, or sprinkled on top of, rye bread loaves. Caraway seeds taste a bit like anise or licorice.

1 TAMARILLO SAUCE
Ecuador

Tamarillos, or tree tomatoes, are small yellow or orange fruits with a tangy flavor that grow on small trees. In Ecuador, they're used to make a spicy sauce, or ají. Other ingredients in the sauce might include hot red chili peppers and cilantro. You'll see this special sauce on just about every table in Ecuador.

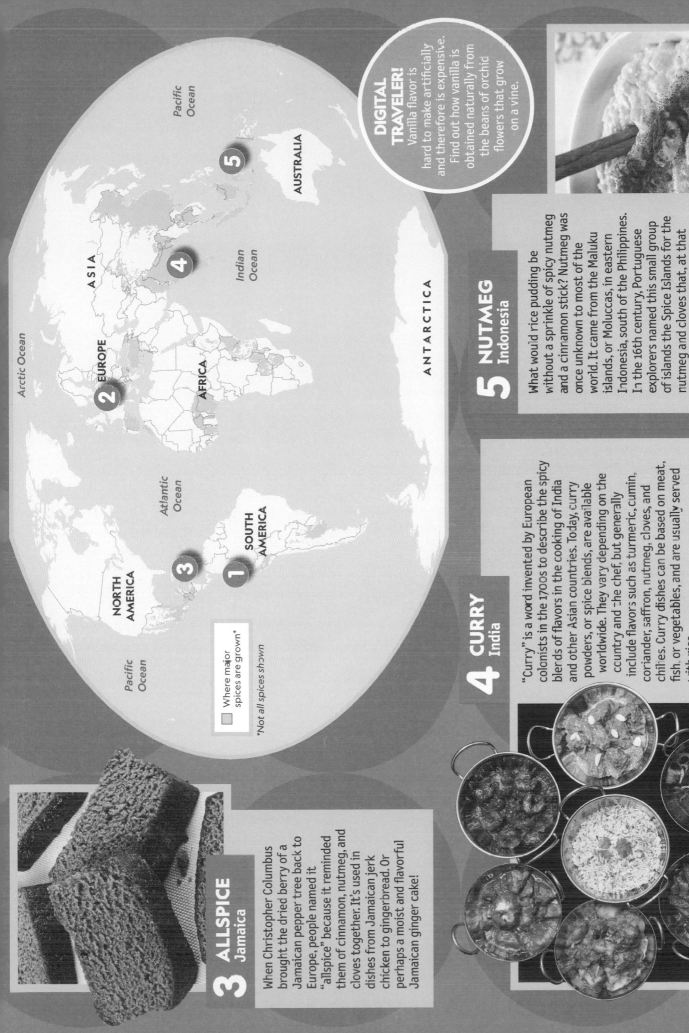

DIGITAL TRAVELER!
Vanilla flavor is hard to make artificially and therefore is expensive. Find out how vanilla is obtained naturally from the beans of orchid flowers that grow on a vine.

Arctic Ocean

NORTH AMERICA

EUROPE

ASIA

Pacific Ocean

AFRICA

Atlantic Ocean

Indian Ocean

Pacific Ocean

SOUTH AMERICA

AUSTRALIA

ANTARCTICA

Where major spices are grown*

*Not all spices shown

3 ALLSPICE
Jamaica

When Christopher Columbus brought the dried berry of a Jamaican pepper tree back to Europe, people named it "allspice" because it reminded them of cinnamon, nutmeg, and cloves together. It's used in dishes from Jamaican jerk chicken to gingerbread. Or perhaps a moist and flavorful Jamaican ginger cake!

4 CURRY
India

"Curry" is a word invented by European colonists in the 1700s to describe the spicy blends of flavors in the cooking of India and other Asian countries. Today, curry powders, or spice blends, are available worldwide. They vary depending on the country and the chef, but generally include flavors such as turmeric, cumin, coriander, saffron, nutmeg, cloves, and chilies. Curry dishes can be based on meat, fish, or vegetables, and are usually served with rice.

5 NUTMEG
Indonesia

What would rice pudding be without a sprinkle of spicy nutmeg and a cinnamon stick? Nutmeg was once unknown to most of the world. It came from the Maluku islands, or Moluccas, in eastern Indonesia, south of the Philippines. In the 16th century, Portuguese explorers named this small group of islands the Spice Islands for the nutmeg and cloves that, at that time, were found only there.

AUSTRALIA AND OCEANIA

FEASTING off the LAND and SEA

Australia, the smallest continent, is also a country. Because it's in the Southern Hemisphere, its northern coast—closer to the Equator—is tropical. Sugarcane and tropical fruits such as bananas and mangoes are produced in the northeast. The south of Australia has a mild climate, good for producing wheat and other grains. The interior, or outback, is largely desert. About 1,300 miles (2,092 km) east of Australia is New Zealand, a lush green country known for its many sheep. Thousands of other islands of Oceania are scattered to the north and east across the Pacific. On these islands, coconuts, papayas, and many other tropical fruits thrive, and fresh seafood is plentiful.

Family members rest in their kitchen garden in a village on Papua New Guinea.

FOODIE HOT SPOTS

 APPLES ABOUND

Visit the "Apple Isle," the Australian island of Tasmania, where apple trees thrive.

 KUMARA TUBERS

On New Zealand's North Island, sample kumara—a type of sweet potato.

 PICK UP A PAWPAW

On Papua New Guinea, try a smoothie or ice cream made from pawpaw fruit.

 BANANA FESTIVAL

Eat a snack at the Talofofo Banana Festival at Guam's Ipan Beach Park every April.

 GREAT GRAINS

Australia is a top wheat producer and exports wheat throughout Southeast Asia.

 GRILLED SAUSAGES

Australians love to cook sausages made of a variety of meats on barbecue grills.

 BLUE CHEESE

Try some of New Zealand's prize-winning creamy blue cheeses.

 WRAPPED-UP CRABS

On the Solomon Islands, shellfish are wrapped in leaves and baked on hot stones.

 CRACK COCONUTS

Micronesian islands are a source of coconuts, harvested for their flesh, milk, and oil.

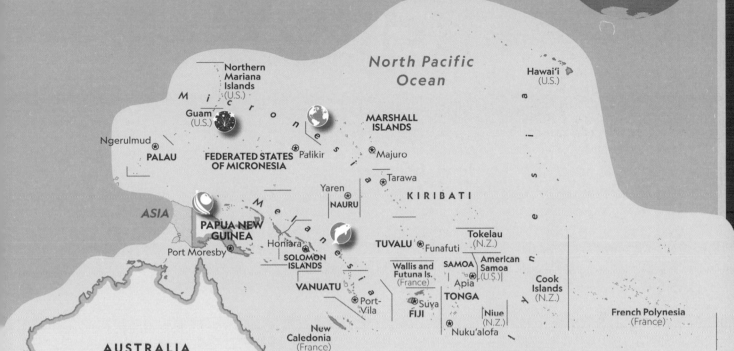

FAST FACTS

Continent size ranking: Seventh largest
Number of countries: 14
Total population: 38,004,000
Largest country by area: Australia

North Pacific Ocean

Hawai'i (U.S.)

Northern Mariana Islands (U.S.)

Micronesia

Guam (U.S.)

MARSHALL ISLANDS

Ngerulmud ⊛

PALAU

FEDERATED STATES OF MICRONESIA

Palikir ⊛

⊛ Majuro

⊛ Tarawa

Yaren ⊛
NAURU

KIRIBATI

ASIA

Melanesia

PAPUA NEW GUINEA

Honiara

Port Moresby

SOLOMON ISLANDS

VANUATU

Port-Vila ⊛

New Caledonia (France)

TUVALU

⊛ Funafuti

Tokelau (N.Z.)

Wallis and Futuna Is. (France)

SAMOA

Apia ⊛

American Samoa (U.S.)

TONGA

Suva ⊛
FIJI

Nuku'alofa ⊛

Niue (N.Z.)

Cook Islands (N.Z.)

French Polynesia (France)

Polynesia

AUSTRALIA

Canberra ⊛

South Pacific Ocean

Indian Ocean

Tasman Sea

NEW ZEALAND

Wellington ⊛

POLITICAL MAP
⊛ National capital

0   800 miles
0   800 kilometers

AUNT BERTHA'S FOOD TRAVEL TIPS

* In Australia and Oceania, you'll have a chance to sample just-caught fish and seafood, and maybe to try catching your own. It's great to know exactly where your food came from!

* If you haven't eaten fresh coconut, Oceania is a good place to try! To open one, you'll need an adult assistant and some tools—a screwdriver to poke holes to drain the coconut milk, a hammer to break the shell, and a vegetable peeler to remove the flesh.

* Australians are famous for their love of barbecues. Enjoy a picnic and do some barbecuing on the many grills available in public parks and on beaches. Just bring your own snags (sausages).

? DID YOU KNOW?

Oceania is a region of the Central and South Pacific Ocean. It includes the big islands of Australia and New Zealand; Papua New Guinea; and three regions of small islands—Melanesia, Micronesia, and Polynesia. The islands of Hawaii— a U.S. state—are part of Polynesia.

ISLAND GROWN

REMOTE RANCHES and tropical FRUITS

Australian sugarcane harvest

Australia is home to productive vegetable farms, wheat fields, dairy farms, and remote cattle stations (ranches). In New Zealand, farmers raise grains, vegetables, and plenty of sheep. Many people in Oceania practice subsistence farming, growing just enough in their gardens for themselves and their families—instead of the commercial farming found elsewhere. Favorite crops include yams, sweet potatoes, and taros. And, of course, fresh fruits of many kinds grow on the tropical islands.

5 COOL FOODS

1 BREADFRUIT
Papua New Guinea

The breadfruit, believed to be native to this island, is now grown in many tropical areas. A ripe fruit tastes like fresh-baked bread, and it's packed with nutrients. Unripe breadfruit is cooked and used like a vegetable.

DIGITAL TRAVELER!
The Tok Pisin language, used throughout Papua New Guinea, includes many words that sound similar to English words. Can you figure out the English translations for the *pinat* and *kukamba* crops?

2 LEATHERWOOD HONEY
Australia

During six weeks from January to March, leatherwood trees bloom in the rainforests of Tasmania. During this season, beekeepers take their beehives full of bees and move into camps in the ancient wilderness of western Tasmania. The bees collect nectar from the leatherwood flowers and bring it back to the hives, where they make a honey with a distinctive spicy taste. It is made only in Tasmania but is exported widely.

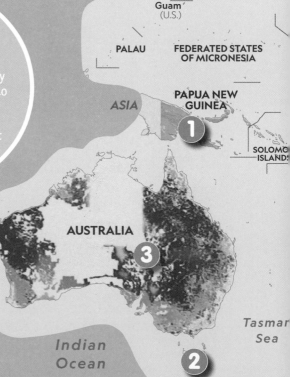

Northern Mariana Islands (U.S.)

Guam (U.S.)

PALAU

FEDERATED STATES OF MICRONESIA

ASIA

PAPUA NEW GUINEA

1

SOLOMON ISLANDS

AUSTRALIA

3

Indian Ocean

Tasman Sea

2

3 BEEF
Australia

Outback cattle stations raise one of Australia's most important foods: beef. Australians eat their beef in sausages, hamburgers, steaks, meat pies, and more. The cattle stations are huge. The largest, Anna Creek Station, is bigger than the country of Belize.

4 PINEAPPLES
Hawaii, U.S.A.

Pineapples, native to South America, were imported to the Hawaiian Islands by European settlers. By the 1960s, Hawaii was growing, canning, and exporting 80 percent of the world's canned pineapples. Try the many ways pineapples are eaten on the islands.

APPETIZING ATTRACTIONS

FARM OR STATION STAYS

Visitors are welcome to spend the night at many Australian cattle and sheep stations (ranches). On the Northern Territory's enormous Bullo River Station, you'll see flat landscapes covered with cattle, rivers filled with crocodiles, and jagged hills decorated with ancient rock art.

PINEAPPLE FARM TOUR

Visit the Dole Plantation in Wahiawa, Oahu, Hawaii, U.S.A. Take a train tour, hear about the history of pineapples, or try your luck in a garden maze. You can also try a Dole Whip, a tasty frozen dessert.

EKASUP CULTURAL VILLAGE

In the island nation of Vanuatu, visit Ekasup Village on the island of Efate for a glimpse into Melanesian culture. Villagers demonstrate traditional farming and cooking, and visitors can sample local fruits and nuts.

? DID YOU KNOW?

On Pohnpei, in the Federated States of Micronesia, local people have many names for yams, and they compete to grow the largest yam tuber. The tubers can grow so large that it takes several people to carry one!

AUSTRALIA AND OCEANIA

North Pacific Ocean

Hawai'i
(U.S.)

4

MARSHALL ISLANDS

NAURU

KIRIBATI

TUVALU

Tokelau
(N.Z.)

Wallis and Futuna Is.
(France)

SAMOA

American Samoa
(U.S.)

VANUATU

TONGA

FIJI

Niue
(N.Z.)

Cook Islands
(N.Z.)

French Polynesia
(France)

New Caledonia
(France)

South Pacific Ocean

NEW ZEALAND

5

FARMLAND USAGE

Pasture ▬▬▬ Cropland

☐ Other land use

5 SHEEP
New Zealand

In 1773, British captain James Cook released two sheep in New Zealand. Soon after, more sheep were released. A century later, sheep farming was going strong. In fact, this country is home to many more sheep than people! Sheep are raised for wool, milk, and meat.

5 COOL FOODS

1 PALUSAMI
Samoa

These bundles of taro leaves are a traditional Samoan favorite. Taro leaves are stuffed with a mixture of coconut milk, vegetables, and seasonings such as onions and chilies. Sometimes fish, chicken, or canned corned beef is added.

DIGITAL TRAVELER!

Vegemite may sound like a vegetable, but this beloved Australian food paste—eaten spread on toast—comes from something else. Grab an adult and go online to find out what! Then compare it with the United Kingdom's Marmite.

VEGEMITE
KRAFT
115 g e
YEAST EXTRACT

Map

North Pacific Ocean

Hawai'i (U.S.)

Northern Mariana Islands (U.S.)

Guam (U.S.)

MARSHALL ISLANDS

ROOTS and TUBERS PRODUCTION*
U.S. tons per acre (metric tons per hectare)

■ More than 5.7 (12.7)
■ 5.7 (12.7) or less
□ 0

*Not all roots and tubers shown

PALAU

FEDERATED STATES OF MICRONESIA

ASIA

KIRIBATI

PAPUA NEW GUINEA

3

NAURU

SOLOMON ISLANDS

5

TUVALU

Tokelau (N.Z.)

SAMOA

1

American Samoa (U.S.)

VANUATU

Wallis and Futuna Is. (France)

FIJI

Niue (N.Z.)

Cook Islands (N.Z.)

French Polynesia (France)

New Caledonia (France)

TONGA

AUSTRALIA

4

South Pacific Ocean

Indian Ocean

Tasman Sea

NEW ZEALAND

2

2 WARRIGAL GREENS
New Zealand

Warrigal greens, native to New Zealand and Australia, are sometimes called New Zealand spinach. They're the leaves of a wild plant that grows well in harsh conditions. Mild, tasty, and a little salty, the leaves are good used in a stir-fry or a salad, or with feta cheese in a quiche.

3 SAGO
Papua New Guinea

Sago is the starchy inner tissue of the sago palm that grows on Papua New Guinea and on nearby islands. The tissue is removed from trees and used in soups, puddings, bread, noodles, and biscuits.

a fruit and vegetable market on Vanuatu

FRESHLY PICKED

Starchy SAGOS, TAROS, and WILD GREENS

Much of the traditional diet in Oceania is based on root vegetables—yams, sweet potatoes, taros, cassavas, and more. People also use the leaves of taro, banana, and other plants for wrapping and cooking foods. Australia grows many vegetable crops, and veggies are available fresh, frozen, or canned. Most of Australia's vegetable crops were introduced there from Europe and elsewhere, though some sweet potatoes, fruits, spices, and greens are indigenous to down under.

4 BEETS
Australia

In Melbourne, you'll want to top your hamburger with a nice big slice of ... canned beet! It's one of the most popular burger toppings in Australia, along with canned pineapple and fried.

5 CASSAVA PUDDING
Solomon Islands

The cassava plant, originally from South America, has become a staple in much of Oceania. The tuber, a part of the cassava root, is used to make a pudding. The roots are grated and mixed with brown sugar, coconut milk, and cinnamon, then baked in banana leaves.

APPETIZING ATTRACTIONS

↘ ROOFTOP FARMING
In Perth, on Australia's western coast, visit the QV1 rooftop garden. Office workers in the building tend vegetable gardens with the help of the staff and volunteers of the nonprofit Perth City Farm, which works to make the city more sustainable.

↘ HUNT FOR TRUFFLES
At the Truffle Farm in Canberra, Australia, you can join truffle-hunting dogs to search for the elusive tasty underground fungus among the trees. When a dog finds one, you can help dig it up and then enjoy a truffle tasting at the farm. Truffles have a strong earthy taste and are used to flavor dishes such as pasta or scrambled eggs.

↘ NIGHT MARKET
On Rarotonga, in the Cook Islands, visit the outdoor Night Market at Muri Beach for free entertainment and a huge variety of fresh local foods, offered by different vendors every night. Have a seat at a picnic table to taste your selections and chat with some locals!

🏆 RECORD BREAKER
Saffron is a spice obtained from threads within flowers of the saffron crocus. It is the world's most expensive spice, costing $5,000 or more per pound (.45 kg) of threads. The saffron crocus, believed to be native to Greece and long grown in Iran and India, is also cultivated in Australia and New Zealand.

AUSTRALIA AND OCEANIA

TROPICAL TASTES

tropical fruits

KIWIS, coconuts, pineapples, and PAPAYAS

Tropical fruits grow in much of Oceania, and many of the local dishes include fresh fruit. On Papua New Guinea alone, you could pick about 100 different kinds of edible fruits. And coconut shows up in many dishes. Australia and New Zealand also grow some nuts, legumes including beans, and various fruits. Some fruits, including papayas, bananas, breadfruits, pineapples, chili peppers, and coconuts, can be enjoyed year-round. Others, like squashes, limes, lychees, melons, and many nuts and berries, can be picked and eaten only at the end of their growing season.

Northern Mariana Islands (U.S.)

Guam (U.S.) **5**

PALAU   FEDERATED STATES OF MICRONESIA

ASIA   PAPUA NEW GUINEA   **3**

SOLOMON ISLAND

AUSTRALIA   **1**

Indian Ocean

Tasman Sea

5 COOL FOODS

1 MACADAMIA NUTS
Australia

Macadamia nuts are native to the forests of Queensland and New South Wales in eastern Australia. They add a rich taste and nice crunch to breads, sweets, and meat dishes. You can also pop them in your mouth raw.

2 KIWI
New Zealand

This odd-looking fruit with a fuzzy brown outside and tart, seedy green inside originated in China. Buy one, cut it open, and scoop out the flesh to eat. The flesh makes a colorful smoothie, and kiwi slices make nice decorations for desserts and other dishes.

? DID YOU KNOW?

A breadfruit tree can live for 80 years and produce about 250 fruits a year. So one breadfruit tree can feed a family for many years. The fruits can be eaten as a starter, as a starch (like a potato), or as a sweet dessert.

3 PAPAYA
Papua New Guinea

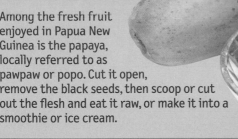

Among the fresh fruit enjoyed in Papua New Guinea is the papaya, locally referred to as pawpaw or popo. Cut it open, remove the black seeds, then scoop or cut out the flesh and eat it raw, or make it into a smoothie or ice cream.

APPETIZING ATTRACTIONS

➤ TROPICAL GARDEN
Vanilla flavor comes from the beans of orchids growing as vines. Visit the Moorea Tropical Garden in French Polynesia to see vanilla vines, breadfruit trees, pineapples, and more.

➤ TE VARA NUI VILLAGE
Visit the Coconut Hut, where guides demonstrate how to climb a tree to pick a coconut and husk the raw fruit. This cultural village on Rarotonga introduces guests to the culture of the Cook Islands' Maori. The Maori people here have common ancestors with the Maori of New Zealand, but also cultural differences. Maori lived in the Cook Islands hundreds of years before some migrated to settle in New Zealand about 1,000 years ago.

➤ BYRON BAY
Climb the lighthouse steps above this bay in New South Wales, Australia, for a view of the forests where wild macadamia nuts grow. Visit the nearby farmers market to discover many creative uses for macadamia nuts in pastas, breads, spreads, and more.

North Pacific Ocean

Hawai'i (U.S.)

MARSHALL ISLANDS

AURU

KIRIBATI

TUVALU

Tokelau (N.Z.)

Wallis and Futuna Is. (France)

SAMOA

American Samoa (U.S.)

VANUATU

TONGA

Cook Islands (N.Z.)

Tahiti **4**

FIJI

Niue (N.Z.)

New Caledonia (France)

French Polynesia (France)

South Pacific Ocean

NEW ZEALAND **2**

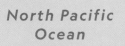

FRUIT PRODUCTION*
U.S. tons per acre
(metric tons per hectare)

■ More than 10.7 (24)
■ 10.7 (24) or less
□ 0

Not all fruits shown

4 PO'E
French Polynesia

This favorite island dessert on Tahiti, French Polynesia, is made with pureed bananas, sugar, and coconut cream, placed in a mold or wrapped in banana leaves, and baked.

AUSTRALIA AND OCEANIA

5 KELAGUEN
Guam

Fruit plays a role in not only sweet desserts, but also in flavoring other dishes. In Guam, people make kelaguen with beef or chicken and a combination of lemon juice, grated coconut, hot peppers, and other fruity seasonings.

DIGITAL TRAVELER!
Marinating fish in the juice of a citrus fruit like lemon or lime "cooks" the fish, just as if it were heated. Grab an adult and go online to learn how the acidic juice changes the texture and taste of the fish.

Easter Island ceviche

CULTURE AND CUISINE

FOOD FAIRS, harvest offerings, and PARADES

DIGITAL TRAVELER!
Find out about remote, volcanic Easter Island in Polynesia, the Tapati Festival held there every February, and ceviche, a traditional local seafood dish prepared and eaten at the event.

From traditional feasts celebrating local cultures to fairs where local farmers and vendors show off their wares, in Australia and Oceania you'll find plenty of places to enjoy festive foods. Some islands, including Hawaii, lie north of the Equator, but most of Oceania is in the Southern Hemisphere, where summer starts in December and winter begins in June. Colorful festivals celebrate foods across the Pacific Ocean and through the seasons.

1 MAKAHIKI
Hawaii, U.S.A.

In ancient Hawaii, Makahiki was a four-month festival (from late October to February) that celebrated the New Year and the harvest and honored Lono, the god of agriculture. On the island of Oahu, Waimea Valley hosts a modern-day celebration that includes exchanges between communities of harvest foods in bundles of ti plant leaves.

2 WILDFOODS FESTIVAL
New Zealand

In March, the town of Hokitika on the west coast of New Zealand's South Island hosts this festival to showcase regional foods. Among the offerings are seagull eggs, possum cutlets, earthworms, snails, and huhu beetle grubs.

PO'E DESSERT

We've used bananas for this dessert, but you can use any tropical fruit or a mix of fruits.

Prep time: 10 minutes; cooking time: 35–45 minutes
Serves: 4–6 people

8 very ripe bananas
½ cup brown sugar
1 cup cornstarch
2 teaspoons vanilla extract
1 tablespoon butter
coconut cream or coconut ice cream

1 Preheat your oven to 375°F.
2 Peel the bananas and cut them into chunks.
3 With an adult's help, puree the banana chunks in a blender or food processor.
4 In a large bowl, mix together the brown sugar, cornstarch, and vanilla with a spoon. Add this mixture to the bananas and puree again until there are no lumps.
5 Grease a 2-quart baking dish with the butter. Pour in the banana mixture.
6 Bake for 35–45 minutes, or until the pudding is firm. Remove it from the oven and allow it to cool.
7 Cover the dish with foil or a clean dish towel and refrigerate it for 2–3 hours.
8 Cut the po'e into squares. Top with coconut cream or coconut ice cream.

3 NIGHT NOODLE MARKETS
Australia

The Enlighten Festival, held in Australia's capital of Canberra, celebrates Australia's autumn (in March) by illuminating the capital's buildings with colorful projected images. It also celebrates its Asian community, holding Night Noodle Markets that offer a variety of noodles and other Asian foods.

5 COOL FOOD EVENTS

① Hawaii, U.S.A.
② New Zealand
③ Australia
④ Tahiti
⑤ Federated States of Micronesia

4 'URU FESTIVAL
French Polynesia

In February or March, the town of Papeete on the island of Tahiti in French Polynesia hosts a weekend celebration of local fruits and other produce, in particular the favorite breadfruit, or 'uru, with recipes, tastings, and cooking demonstrations.

5 YAP DAY
Micronesia

This March celebration on the island of Yap, in the Federated States of Micronesia, celebrates Yapese culture, customs, and foods, with dancing, crafts, tattoos, cooking demonstrations, and competitions.

AUSTRALIA AND OCEANIA

119

WHEAT AND MORE

grain-bearing ears of wheat

COOKIES, baguettes, cakes, and BAKERIES

Australia grows grains including wheat, barley, corn, and oats in the south and along the eastern and southwestern coasts. New Zealand also produces these grains, mostly on the South Island. In Oceania, starches traditionally came from the roots that grow on the islands—taros, yams, cassavas—rather than cereals. But in recent decades, rice from Asia has become popular here. Some farmers in Papua New Guinea started growing rice, but most rice in Oceania is still imported.

APPETIZING ATTRACTIONS

➤ RIDE THE GHAN

A great way to see South Australia's wheat fields is through the windows of a train called the Ghan. Starting in Adelaide in the south, the train heads north through vast wheat fields. It continues 1,851 miles (2,979 km) through desert and sheep and cattle stations (ranches) to Alice Springs, then on to the northern city of Darwin.

➤ PATCHWORK PLAINS

On New Zealand's South Island, take a balloon ride for a bird's-eye view of the enormous Canterbury Plains. This patchwork of farms produces more than 80 percent of New Zealand's grains, seeds, and vegetable crops.

➤ FRENCH BAKERIES

The 100-plus islands of French Polynesia are part of overseas France, and the people born there are French citizens. When visiting islands such as Tahiti, you'll hear French spoken and you'll see bakeries selling fine French baguettes (long, crusty loaves of bread), croissants, and pastries. On smaller islands, bakeries deliver fresh-baked goods to customers' homes.

5 COOL FOODS

1 ANZAC BISCUITS
New Zealand

This cookie has a story! ANZAC stands for the Australian and New Zealand Army Corps, which fought in World War I. These crunchy cookies were created from the limited ingredients available in people's kitchens during the war—oats, flour, sugar, dried coconut, butter, and water. Since the cookies had no eggs, they didn't go bad when soldiers took them along on long sea journeys. Today's Anzac biscuits have a similar recipe.

2 BUCHI BUCHI
Guam

This pastry turnover, filled with sweet pumpkin filling and fried, is a fall favorite in Guam. The rest of the year, this pastry is made using canned rather than fresh pumpkin.

3 COCONUT BREAD
Fiji

A popular Fijian recipe uses fresh coconut and coconut milk to bake a moist, tasty coconut bread, giving this food a tropical flair.

4 PANIPOPO
Samoa

Soft, tender rolls are sweetened with a soaking of coconut sauce to make this popular Samoan dessert. Try it at a seaside café.

North Pacific Ocean

GRAIN PRODUCTION*
U.S. tons per acre
(metric tons per hectare)

More than 0.1 (0.3)
0.1 (0.3) or less
0

*Not all grains shown

Northern Mariana Islands (U.S.)

Hawai'i (U.S.)

Guam (U.S.) **2**

MARSHALL ISLANDS

PALAU

FEDERATED STATES OF MICRONESIA

ASIA

PAPUA NEW GUINEA

NAURU

K I R I B A T I

SOLOMON ISLANDS

TUVALU

Tokelau (N.Z.)

SAMOA

American Samoa (U.S.)

4

Wallis and Futuna Is. (France)

Cook Islands (N.Z.)

VANUATU

3

French Polynesia (France)

Niue (N.Z.)

New Caledonia (France)

FIJI

TONGA

AUSTRALIA

5

South Pacific Ocean

AUSTRALIA AND OCEANIA

Indian Ocean

Tasman Sea

NEW ZEALAND

1

5 LAMINGTON
Australia

Called the national cake of Australia, this square sponge cake is iced with chocolate frosting and coconut flakes and often has jam or cream in the center.

DIGITAL TRAVELER!
Australians love Iced VoVo biscuits. Former prime minster Kevin Rudd even mentioned them in his victory speech. Grab an adult and look online to learn about these sweet treats.

RECORD BREAKER
Australia boasts an international cuisine that features many Asian foods. In 2019, the world's largest ever dim sum meal was served as part of a Lunar New Year celebration in Sydney to ring in the Chinese zodiac Year of the Pig. About 3,100 individual pieces of dim sum were served to 764 diners, free of charge.

5 COOL FOODS

1 PIG ROAST
Papua New Guinea

People on many islands of Oceania create feasts of roast pork. The pig may be cooked whole or in pieces in a traditional earth oven or pit, called a mumu in Papua New Guinea (or an imu elsewhere). Sweet potatoes, other root vegetables, rice, greens, and other dishes often accompany the feast.

North Pacific Ocean

Northern Mariana Islands (U.S.)

Guam (U.S.)

Hawai'i (U.S.) 3

MARSHALL ISLANDS

PALAU

FEDERATED STATES OF MICRONESIA

ASIA

PAPUA NEW GUINEA 1

NAURU

KIRIBATI

SOLOMON ISLANDS

TUVALU

Tokelau (N.Z.)

VANUATU

Wallis and Futuna Is. (France)

SAMOA

American Samoa (U.S.)

5

Cook Islands (N.Z.)

French Polynesia (France)

New Caledonia (France)

FIJI

TONGA

Niue (N.Z.)

AUSTRALIA

2

South Pacific Ocean

Indian Ocean

Tasman Sea

NEW ZEALAND

4

2 EMU
Australia

A meat you might encounter around Sydney is Australia's indigenous alternative to turkey: the ostrichlike emu. Its meat is very low in fat, and has nutrients such as iron. Emu was traditionally eaten by Australia's indigenous people. Today, you might see it as a pizza topping, or in meat pies. Emu eggs are good to eat, too—and just one egg is as much food as 10 chicken eggs!

3 GUAVA CHICKEN
Hawaii, U.S.A.

A popular recipe in Hawaii uses guava juice to spice up grilled chicken. Just mix together guava juice, ketchup, soy sauce, brown sugar, garlic, and Chinese five-spice powder, and soak your chicken pieces in this mixture overnight in the refrigerator. Then grill it for a Hawaiian-style barbecue.

LOCAL MEALS

a witchetty grub larva

DIGITAL TRAVELER!
The Aboriginal people of Australia traditionally roasted plump moth larvae known as witchetty grubs over coals. Find out more about entomophagy—eating insects—and the insects people eat around the world.

From VENISON stew to GUAVA CHICKEN

APPETIZING ATTRACTIONS

Before European explorers arrived, the indigenous peoples of Australia and Oceania relied on native plants and fish for food. Explorers, missionaries, and settlers brought new foods, including chickens, pigs, and lambs, which have been incorporated into local foods and cultures. And, perhaps because the sun shines so often in this part of the world, people do a lot of outdoor cooking!

POLYNESIAN CULTURAL CENTER

This attraction on Oahu, Hawaii, U.S.A., offers visitors the chance to learn about cultural traditions and foods of Polynesia. The festive luau offers traditional foods such as a whole pig roasted in an imu—an underground oven.

ADELAIDE CENTRAL MARKET

This large, colorful indoor market in Adelaide, South Australia, has been selling Australian meats and produce for more than 150 years. Expect a crowd—more than nine million shoppers visit every year.

"SCHOOL OF THE AIR" FOR RANCH KIDS

Australia's beef industry depends on families living in remote areas on gigantic ranches, or cattle stations, many miles from regular schools. Kids who live on cattle stations connect with one another through radio and the internet. Find out more about the School of the Air at its center in Alice Springs.

4 VENISON
New Zealand

Deer were imported to New Zealand for deer hunting in the late 1800s. Facing no predators and plenty of food, the deer multiplied to the point where they damaged the native forests and pastures. Today, more than 1.7 million deer are raised on free-range farms for their meat (known as venison), which is eaten as steaks or in stews.

5 CURRIED CORNED BEEF
Fiji

There aren't a lot of animals raised for meat on Fiji, so people often use canned corned beef to make this dish. The meat is often eaten curried with onion, ginger, and turmeric, and accompanied by carrots or taro root.

! STRANGE BUT TRUE

The largest wild camel herd in the world is in Australia. Camels were introduced into the outback in the 1840s to provide transportation across the enormous stretches of desert.

AUSTRALIA AND OCEANIA

DAIRY DELICIOUS

pavlova

ICE CREAM, puddings, and plenty of CHEESE

Across Oceania's many small islands, the only "milk" traditionally used was the milk from coconuts, though dairy products from cow's milk are now widely available. Likewise, before Europeans and their livestock arrived, the indigenous peoples of Australia and New Zealand didn't have dairy, either. Currently in those nations, dairy farmers raise a range of animals—from cows to camels—for their milk.

DIGITAL TRAVELER!
The pavlova—a whipped-cream dessert with a crisp meringue crust topped with fresh fruit slices—is famous in both New Zealand and Australia. Find out how it got its name and where it originated.

5 COOL FOODS

1 COCONUT MOUSSE
Nauru

When you have a lot of coconuts, why not make coconut mousse? This sweet pudding is a specialty of the Micronesian island of Nauru. It uses fresh coconut, sugar, vanilla, heavy cream, which is whipped, and coconut milk, which is not. Egg whites are folded in, making an airy dessert. The mix is chilled before eating.

Northern Mariana Islands (U.S.)

Guam (U.S.)

MARSHALL ISLANDS

PALAU

FEDERATED STATES OF MICRONESIA

ASIA

PAPUA NEW GUINEA

1 NAURU

K

SOLOMON ISLANDS

TUVALU

Wallis and Futuna Is. (France)

VANUATU

FIJI

AUSTRALIA

2 **4**

New Caledonia (France)

South Pacific

Indian Ocean

Tasman Sea

NEW ZEALAND

3 **5**

2 CAMEL'S MILK CHEESE
Australia

Creative foodies in Australia have transformed camel's milk into tasty gelato, soft cheeses such as Halloumi and feta, and even milk chocolate. If you live in Australia, you can sign up for regular deliveries from the farm!

3 HOKEY POKEY ICE CREAM
New Zealand

This ice-cream flavor was invented in New Zealand and is so popular there that in 1994 it was printed on a postage stamp. It's vanilla ice cream with bits of "hokey pokey" (crunchy, gooey honeycomb toffee candy) mixed in.

New Zealand 45c
KIWIANA
HOKEY POKEY ICE CREAM

RECORD BREAKER

Cowaramup, in Western Australia, is a real cow town, and its residents aren't afraid to show how much they like their cows. In 2014, 1,352 people dressed up in black-and-white cow onesies—and smashed the world record for largest gathering of people dressed as cows.

4 CHEESE-FILLED DAMPER
Australia

In the 1800s in Australia's outback, road workers and settlers made a simple bread they called damper. The dough—a mixture of flour, water, and a little salt—was shaped into a disk and baked in campfire coals. Today's cooks bake a variation with a cheesy center, adding mozzarella and cheddar cheeses. Sometimes, they also add oats.

5 SHEEP'S MILK CHEESE
New Zealand

Some dairy farmers in New Zealand milk sheep, making yogurt and cheeses from sheep's milk. Each cheese may have a rind, or covering, of a certain color and flavor. Try a sample at a food stall or farmers market.

Map labels

North Pacific Ocean

Hawai'i (U.S.)

RIBATI

Tokelau (N.Z.)

SAMOA | American Samoa (U.S.)

Cook Islands (N.Z.)

Niue (N.Z.)

TONGA

French Polynesia (France)

Ocean

MILK PRODUCTION
U.S. tons per acre
(metric tons per hectare)

- More than 0.1 (0.2)
- 0.02–0.1 (0.05–0.2)
- 0.01–0.02 (0.03–0.05)
- 0.004–0.009 (0.01–0.02)
- Less than 0.004 (0.01)
- No data

APPETIZING ATTRACTIONS

↳ HONOLULU ICE CREAM

Under the hot Hawaiian sun, an ice-cream cone can hit the spot. Honolulu shops offer a huge selection of flavors, often from local ingredients. Look for ice-cream flavors like avocado, pineapple, or pizza. Or try mochi—ice cream wrapped in a sweet rice cake.

↳ VISIT A CAMEL FARM

In Kyabram, Victoria, Australia, visit the Camel Milk Co Australia farm and meet the camels up close and personal. You can even feed them by hand. And don't forget to taste camel's milk and milk products.

↳ CHECK OUT A CHEESERY

At the north end of New Zealand's North Island, visit Mahoe Cheese, near Kerikeri. This family business raises a herd of cows, makes prize-winning cheeses, and welcomes visitors to stop by and have a taste.

AUSTRALIA AND OCEANIA

125

SEAFOOD DELIGHTS

From FISH fritters to Balmain BUGS

Australians along the coasts take full advantage of the fresh seafood available to them. On the islands of Oceania, men and women continue traditional fishing practices. Across the continent, freshwater lakes and streams offer other tasty local options. Batter-fried fish, grilled crustaceans, and succulent seaweed are just some of the dishes made from this region's seafood.

Polynesian fishers

5 COOL FOODS

1 BUGS
Australia

In Australia, local species of lobsters are the Moreton Bay Bug and Balmain Bug. Unlike other types of lobsters, these flat-shaped crustaceans do not have big claws, and only their tail meat is edible. Grilled with herb and garlic butter, you'll find these seafood bugs served at picnics and in fine restaurants.

2 KOKODA
Fiji

Any fresh, locally caught fish, such as mahi mahi, can be turned into kokoda. Just marinate it in citrus juices and mix it with some coconut cream, onions, tomatoes, and chilies. This favorite festive dish is often served in a large clamshell or coconut shell.

DIGITAL TRAVELER!
Throughout Oceania, oysters are raised at seafood farms. Find out how these shellfish grow and are harvested and the ways they are cooked and eaten.

APPETIZING ATTRACTIONS

GIANT CLAM FARM
In Lelu, on Kosrae island, the Micronesia Management and Marketing Enterprises (MMME) facility raises rare giant clams, which can grow to four feet (1.2 m) long! Raising these giant shellfish on farms, rather than disturbing wild populations, makes for more sustainable seafood populations. Visit the facility for a tour and close-up view of the clams.

FISH MARKET
On the Micronesian island of Pohnpei, look for small roadside markets selling fresh-caught fish, crabs, lobsters, and other local foods.

TROUT CENTER
In New Zealand, visit the Tongariro National Trout Centre, near Lake Taupo. It offers young fishers the chance to fish for rainbow trout in a special, kids-only trout pond, and then get their catch smoked for a family picnic.

AMOUNT OF FISH CAUGHT

Average pounds (kilograms)
per person per year

■	More than 132 (60)
■	68–132 (31–60)
■	46–67 (21–30)
□	11–45 (5–20)
□	Less than 11 (5)

North Pacific Ocean

Hawai'i (U.S.)

French Polynesia (France)

Tahiti

5

Cook Islands (N.Z.)

Tokelau (N.Z.)

American Samoa (U.S.)

SAMOA

Niue (N.Z.)

TONGA

Wallis and Futuna Is. (France)

FIJI

2 **3**

TUVALU

K I R I B A T I

MARSHALL ISLANDS

NAURU

SOLOMON ISLANDS

VANUATU

New Caledonia (France)

South Pacific Ocean

NEW ZEALAND

4

Tasman Sea

Northern Mariana Islands (U.S.)

Guam (U.S.)

FEDERATED STATES OF MICRONESIA

PALAU

ASIA

PAPUA NEW GUINEA

AUSTRALIA

1

Indian Ocean

3 SEA GRAPE SALAD
Fiji

The seaweed called nama in Fiji is known as sea grapes, or even green caviar, elsewhere in the world. The little bubbles of green on this algae are soft but pleasantly crunchy when eaten. Nama is usually eaten topped with lemon juice or a little coconut cream as part of a fresh salad.

4 WHITEBAIT FRITTERS
New Zealand

This fish dish specialty of New Zealand is made using tiny freshwater fish such as inanga or other fresh catch from local rivers. The fish are cooked with eggs and butter and served with lemon. There's a friendly competition between North Island and South Island folks as to who has the better recipe.

? DID YOU KNOW?

In Polynesia, people have practiced "stone fishing" for hundreds of years. People beat the water with stones to make the fish move. Fishers herd the fish toward the shore and corral them in netting made of palm fronds. Edible fish are harvested, and the rest are released.

5 POISSON CRU
French Polynesia

This island specialty is freshly caught raw fish, usually tuna, diced and marinated in lime. For a Tahitian version of fish-and-chips, try it with a side of taro chips.

5 COOL FOODS

1 COCONUT MACAROONS
Italy

Sweet, golden-baked macaroon cookies were made in Italy in the Middle Ages using almond paste mixed with egg whites and sweetened milk. When shredded coconut flesh was used instead of almond paste around the 1890s, coconut macaroons became a new favorite—and not just in Europe.

2 MOQUECA DE CAMARÃO
Brazil

This zesty Brazilian shrimp stew uses a coconut milk base. Onions, garlic, red peppers, tomatoes, cilantro, chilies, and lime juice may be added to balance the sweet coconut flavor.

Arctic Ocean

NORTH AMERICA

EUROPE

ASIA

Pacific Ocean

Atlantic Ocean

Pacific Ocean

1

4

3

AFRICA

Where coconuts are grown

5

Indian Ocean

SOUTH AMERICA

2

AUSTRALIA

ANTARCTICA

DIGITAL TRAVELER!
Coconut palms spread their seeds far from the tree—even to remote ocean islands. Grab an adult and go online to discover how they do this.

3 TOM KHA GAI
Thailand

Thai coconut chicken soup blends chicken and mushrooms with spicy lemongrass and lime, chilies, and cilantro in coconut milk. The soup is creamy, tangy, salty, and delicious!

coconuts on a palm tree

COCONUT CUISINE

VERSATILE FRUIT of a tropical PALM TREE

Coconut palm trees grow well in tropical and subtropical climates, so you'll see them in parts of Oceania, Asia, Africa, and the Americas. Coconuts are the fruit of these trees. On the tree, the fruits grow to 15 inches (38 cm) long, and have a rough, tough outer husk. When the husk is removed, the large inner seed, or stone, is revealed. This giant seed is what you usually see sold as a fresh coconut in grocery stores.

When a coconut seed is unripe, it is filled with coconut water, a liquid often enjoyed as a refreshing drink. When the seed is ripe, its hard, thick shell is lined with sweet, crunchy white meat, or flesh, also called the kernel. Coconut meat can be sliced or shredded. It's good to eat raw, and is often dried to use in baking. Pressing the coconut meat produces coconut oil, which is also used for cooking. Coconut meat and oil are tasty ingredients in dishes ranging from spicy soups to sweet desserts. They're also good sources of vitamins and minerals.

4 GERMAN CHOCOLATE CAKE
United States

This layer cake is from Texas, U.S.A., not Germany! The recipe was first printed in a Dallas newspaper in 1957. It's named for the baking chocolate used, which was invented by Sam German. But the all-important frosting—with chopped pecans and grated coconut flesh—is what makes this cake!

5 KUKU PAKA
Kenya

In Kenya and other East African countries, sample kuku paka—grilled chicken in a coconut curry sauce. Coconut milk or cream and garlic, ginger, tomatoes, lemon, coriander, and curry powder make the sauce spicy and flavorsome! Kuku paka is usually served with steamed rice.

TRUE OR FALSE?

Which of these statements about coconuts are true and which are false?

1. Coconut oil is excellent for cooking, moisturizing dry skin, and lubricating your bicycle.
2. In Thailand, people use specially trained monkeys to harvest coconuts from trees.
3. A coconut is not a nut, but rather a fruit with a stone, similar to a plum or an olive.
4. The best way to get milk from a coconut is to squeeze it.
5. The Fiji flag features a coconut palm.

See answers on page 150.

OCEANS

A HUGE, rich, varied FOOD RESOURCE

Earth's oceans cover about 70 percent of the planet's surface. These waters are home to many plants and animals, some of which are important food sources for people around the world. Popular seafoods include fish of all sizes, crustaceans, mollusks, and seaweeds.

Global demand for seafood is increasing. Modern technology makes it easier for commercial fishers to catch large amounts of fish or shellfish. This can lead to problems. Scientists worry that people are removing fish and other animals from the sea so quickly that certain species could die out. That's why sustainable fishing practices—those that allow fish populations to remain stable—are important. In the past few decades, many commercial fishers have started to adhere to regulations concerning the number of fish that can be caught, for example. Some countries have designated certain protected waters, where fishing is not allowed, to allow fish populations to recover.

You can help make sure your fish is caught through sustainable practices. Learn about the seafood you're eating, where it came from, and how it's caught. When you shop, you can look for labels that identify sustainably harvested seafood. In restaurants, you can ask how the seafood was caught, and eat only selections caught sustainably. By making such choices, you can help protect the future of our fish, our oceans, and our planet.

FOODIE HOT SPOTS

PACIFIC OCEAN

Warm, tropical Pacific waters are home to albacore and skipjack tuna, which can be caught sustainably with a fishing pole and line. Tuna, which is rich in nutrients, can be cooked many ways or eaten raw, such as in Japanese sushi dishes. Seafood provides a large proportion of the animal protein in the diet of people living on small islands in the Pacific.

FAST FACTS

Pacific Ocean area: 69,000,000 square miles (178,800,000 sq km)
Atlantic Ocean area: 35,400,000 square miles (91,700,000 sq km)
Arctic Ocean area: 5,600,000 square miles (14,700,000 sq km)
Indian Ocean area: 29,400,000 square miles (76,200,000 sq km)

NORTH AMERICA

NORTH PACIFIC OCEAN

EQUATOR

SOUTH PACIFIC OCEAN

AUNT BERTHA'S FOOD TRAVEL TIPS

* When you go to the beach, bring home all of your trash to keep the waters clean. Sea creatures may mistake floating plastic bags for food. Fishing line and packaging can cut and endanger ocean wildlife.

* Check out local fishing boats to see what the crews are hauling in daily or, if permitted, drop a line in the water yourself. Some restaurants near the ocean will even cook your catch for you.

* Eat invasive seafood species to help protect native species. Examples are lionfish in the Caribbean and blue catfish in the Chesapeake Bay.

ATLANTIC OCEAN

The cool waters of the Atlantic Ocean are the perfect habitat for clams, cockles, and mussels, all of which are farmed sustainably in most regions. These shellfish are a tasty treat in soups or served raw on the half shell. Fish harvested sustainably from the Atlantic include salmon and albacore tuna, but check on their status and sustainability as stocks vary over several years.

ARCTIC OCEAN

Along the Arctic Ocean coasts of North America, Asia, and Europe, fishers compete with seals and grizzly bears when fishing for hearty wild salmon and char that swim in rivers leading into the ocean. Offshore, commercial fishing is heavily restricted. While there are still wild fish to be caught, more are sustainably farmed in offshore fish farms to meet the demands of diners from all over the world.

INDIAN OCEAN

People raise fish sustainably in fish farms along Indian Ocean coasts. To catch fish in a sustainable manner in the wild, they use spears or cast nets—small nets thrown into the water by hand. Barramundi is a coastal species widely harvested here. This fish is hatched and grown in a nursery on land and then released into an offshore marine net pen. Barramundi can be steamed, baked, fried, or barbecued.

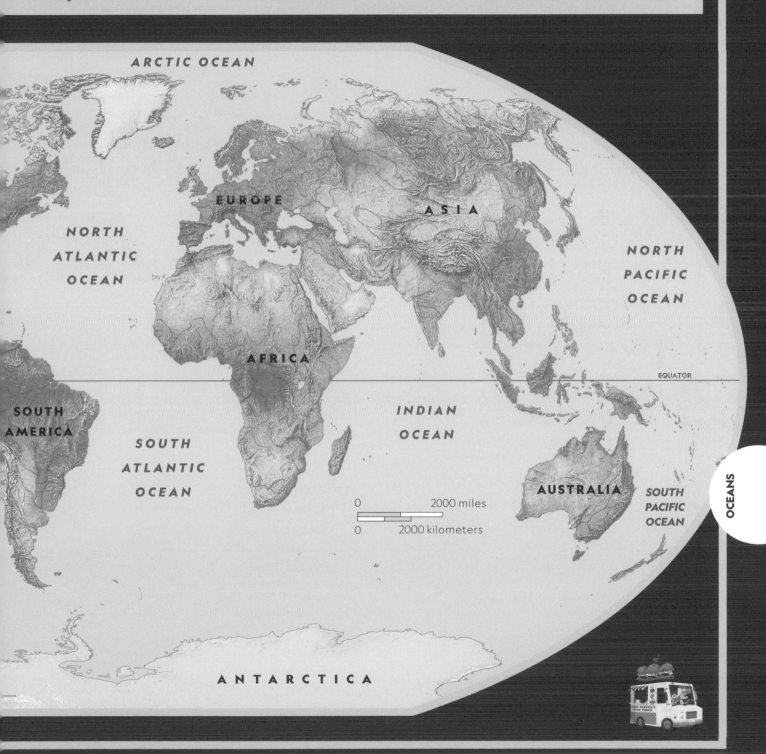

ARCTIC OCEAN

EUROPE

ASIA

NORTH ATLANTIC OCEAN

NORTH AMERICA

NORTH PACIFIC OCEAN

AFRICA

EQUATOR

SOUTH AMERICA

SOUTH ATLANTIC OCEAN

INDIAN OCEAN

AUSTRALIA

SOUTH PACIFIC OCEAN

0   2000 miles

0   2000 kilometers

ANTARCTICA

OCEANS

FOOD FROM THE WATERS

SEAFOOD CATCH

a German shrimp-fishing boat

SAVORY DISHES from the SEA

Nearly half of all people in the world depend on seafood as a major source of protein. Today, China leads the world in both eating and exporting fish and shellfish, with Peru, Japan, the United States, Norway, Chile, Indonesia, and Russia close behind. Sustainable practices and clean waters will allow us all to keep dipping into the water for our food. Harvested from cold and warm seas and oceans, fish and shellfish are cooked and eaten in many ways around the world. Try some wherever you travel.

APPETIZING ATTRACTIONS

➥ GO OCEAN FISHING
Take a fishing charter trip from Tenerife in the Canary Islands, one of the greatest areas for marine diversity. Back on shore, try vieja, sama, or cherne fish at a local restaurant.

➥ DIG FOR YOUR DINNER
Go clamming in Maine, U.S.A. You'll need a bucket, a clam rake, and a clam gauge—which is used to measure each clam you find to ensure it meets the minimum two-inch (5-cm)-length guidelines. Always check to make sure your clamming activities follow local conservation rules.

➥ VISIT AN AQUARIUM
On a visit to Polaria, Norway, try to spot a halibut hiding or stare a catfish in the eye at the northernmost aquarium in the world. It is a unique spot to see many of the marine species of the Arctic Sea.

5 COOL FOODS

1 FISH IN CITRUS JUICE
Samoa

Oka i'a is the Samoan version of the traditional Hawaiian poke dish made with fresh raw tuna, but with the addition of some hot spice. Cut pieces of tuna are soaked in lemon or lime juice for up to 60 minutes, depending on how well you want the fish "cooked." Then onion, cucumber, and tomato are added, along with a little chili pepper, to make a tasty fish salad.

2 SHRIMP PATTIES
Guam

On this island territory of the United States, located in the North Pacific Ocean, try buñelos uhang, or shrimp patties. Made by the native Chamorro people and inspired by American fritters, the patties are made with chopped shrimp, vegetables, and a batter mix. Then they're deep fried. Buñelos uhang are popular for celebrations all over the island.

3 SEA TROUT AND FRITTERS
Falkland Islands

Sea trout, either fried or grilled, and a side of fritters or steamed vegetables, is a main meal to enjoy in the Falkland Islands in the South Atlantic Ocean. These islands off the coast of South America are a British overseas territory. You can see the British influence on menus, which feature British-style fish-and-chips and other English fare. Try the variety of fish dishes the islands have to offer.

? DID YOU KNOW?

South Pacific palolo worms are found on coral reefs in certain areas of the South Pacific Ocean. During spring or early summer each year, just after a full moon, adult worms release their tail sections into the water as a way to reproduce. Islanders from the region wade into the water to collect the long, spaghetti-like strands. They fry the strands with eggs, bake them into bread, or sprinkle them raw on toast for a delicious meal.

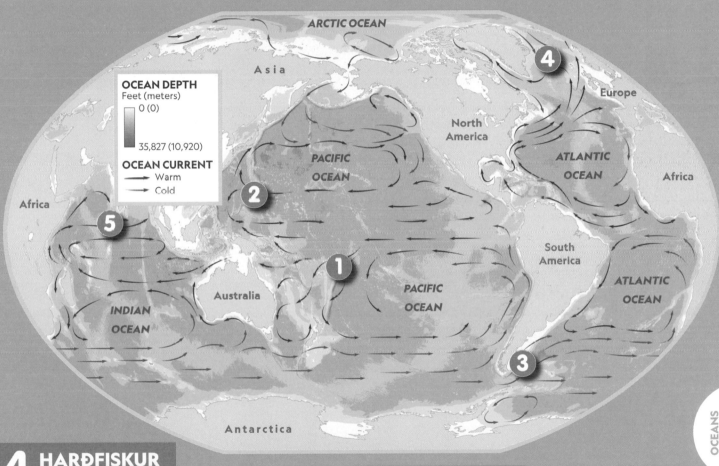

OCEAN DEPTH
Feet (meters)
0 (0)
35,827 (10,920)

OCEAN CURRENT
→ Warm
→ Cold

ARCTIC OCEAN

Asia

North America

Europe

PACIFIC OCEAN

ATLANTIC OCEAN

Africa

Africa

South America

Australia

PACIFIC OCEAN

ATLANTIC OCEAN

INDIAN OCEAN

Antarctica

4 HARÐFISKUR
Iceland

If you like beef jerky, you might just like harðfiskur—a kind of dried fish jerky. Cod, haddock, or wolffish are cut open, gutted, and hung up to dry. Icelanders enjoy it plain or with rich, creamy butter.

5 FISH BREAKFAST
Maldives

Tuna rules in the Maldives, an island nation in the Indian Ocean, where many people eat mas huni—a salad of smoked tuna, coconut, red onion, and chili pepper—often for breakfast.

FEEDING THE WORLD

Providing food for a CHANGING WORLD

Humankind faces many challenges in the battle to feed Earth's ever increasing population. One challenge is climate change. Severe weather events, such as record heat and hurricanes, bring drought and floods, which affect croplands. Warmer global temperatures allow pests, like the mountain pine beetle in the Pacific Northwest region of the United States, to move into areas that were once too cold. Shipping foods all over the world spreads pests, too. And diseases, such as potato blight and wheat leaf rust, continue to harm crops.

Another problem is the increased use of herbicides, pesticides, and fertilizers, which has created superweeds—plants that can withstand large amounts of chemicals and still thrive. The chemicals have also killed plant pollinators, like bees, polluted the soil, and reduced nutrients naturally available to crops.

Fortunately, people around the globe are doing a lot to combat these challenges. To learn about some of these efforts—including recycling water, introducing heirloom varieties, developing genetically modified seeds, and promoting sustainable agricultural practices—keep reading. They're described on pages 136–143.

AUNT BERTHA'S TIPS FOR SUSTAINABLE EATING

* Eat locally grown foods. The more foods you eat that don't use energy in being transported from farms to food stores, the better it is for local farmers, the local economy, and the planet.

* Try eating heirloom produce. These are nutritious but rather uncommon foods that food stores overlook. While offering you unique flavors, they also help preserve biodiversity.

* If you can, try growing your own food, whether it be in a planter, in a vegetable garden, or at a community garden. It will help you discover more about the food you eat and supply you with fresh foods all season.

OVERPOPULATION

More than 7.6 billion people live on Earth—and the population is continuously growing. Estimates are that it will reach 11 billion by the year 2100. As the population increases, so does the need for more food to feed all those people. But with resources like clean groundwater and available farmland decreasing, feeding the world is becoming a bigger challenge for every country, every day.

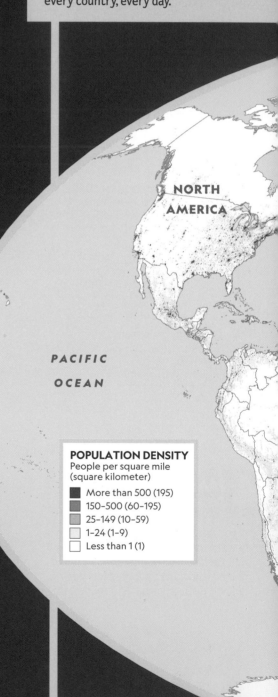

NORTH AMERICA

PACIFIC OCEAN

POPULATION DENSITY
People per square mile
(square kilometer)

- More than 500 (195)
- 150–500 (60–195)
- 25–149 (10–59)
- 1–24 (1–9)
- Less than 1 (1)

CLIMATE CHANGE

Earth's atmosphere is warming due to an increase in the amount of greenhouse gases, such as carbon dioxide, in the air. Most climate scientists agree that human activity is the main cause. This includes energy production, beef production, and transportation. As the atmosphere warms, glaciers melt, sea levels rise, and the environment changes. This causes frequent extreme weather events including droughts, storms, and flooding. These all impact food production and access to clean water.

FOOD SAFETY

In 2018, 62 people in the United States became ill from *E. coli,* probably from contaminated romaine lettuce. This is just one of the increasingly frequent reports of food contamination in the news in recent years. Contaminants include bacteria that make us sick, such as *E. coli* and listeria, as well as chemicals from factories, waste runoff from farms, and even microplastic waste found in fish. Safe food handling and careful agricultural practices are crucial to keeping our food supply healthy.

SOIL NUTRIENTS

Farmers need nutrient-rich topsoil to grow food. But this important layer of soil is disappearing or becoming less usable due to deforestation, pesticide use, rising seas, and record flooding. In addition, overgrazing by farm animals pulls up plants that hold the soil together, allowing topsoil to be washed away with every rain. Some farming practices do not allow farmers to rotate crops, or change the crops they grow every few years so the soil can renew its nutrients. That causes farmers to use more chemicals to grow large crops.

ARCTIC OCEAN

EUROPE

ASIA

WORLD FACTS
World population: 7.6 billion
Most populated country: China, 1,379,303,000
Least populated country: Vatican City, 1,000
Most densely populated country: Macau

ATLANTIC
OCEAN

AFRICA

PACIFIC
OCEAN

INDIAN
OCEAN

SOUTH
AMERICA

AUSTRALIA

ANTARCTICA

FEEDING THE WORLD

FRESH-WATER

a girl drinking from a new well in Uganda

CLEAN water for ALL

Water is the most vital natural resource on Earth. Although the planet is covered in water, about 96.5 percent of it is undrinkable saltwater. Of the 3.5 percent that is freshwater, less than one percent is available as liquid water. The rest is frozen in glaciers and snowfields.

All living things depend on water for survival, but the supply of freshwater is limited, particularly when there is a drought. Despite this, people don't always do a good job of managing this valuable resource. Most freshwater is used for agriculture rather than drinking. And keeping freshwater free from pollution by lead, mercury, oil spills, and sewage is a continuous challenge in a growing world. Recognizing these challenges, people around the world are working to preserve freshwater. Here are five cool projects that are making a positive impact.

2 RECYCLING WATER
United States

Wastewater from homes, schools, and offices is usually cleaned, channeled into rivers, and sent out to sea. This is wasteful in areas where people need water for farming and industry. Advanced water treatment facilities in Southern California are now recycling cleaned wastewater and directing it to farms and factories—in purple pipes, to distinguish them from pipes used for either drinkable or dirty water. Using recycled wastewater for these purposes helps people maintain the drinking water supply.

3 DISASTER AID
Haiti

Supplies of freshwater are often destroyed following natural disasters like hurricanes and earthquakes. In October 2016, Hurricane Matthew disrupted water supplies all over Haiti. International aid groups Pure Water for the World, Norwegian Church Aid, and others immediately set up emergency water supplies there. To prevent the spread of waterborne diseases, they distributed clean-water filters and set up handwashing stations. They also installed rainwater-harvesting systems to help the stricken communities rebuild themselves. Similar aid groups have followed suit and continue to operate globally.

5 COOL PROJECTS

1 DRINKING WATER
India

Working together, the Global Water Project and Wells for Life organizations are funding freshwater well projects in India. Well holes are bored into the earth to reach freshwater located deep in the ground. Then pumps are fitted to draw up the water. The wells are installed in places where people previously had to walk miles to a well in a neighboring village or to a nearby river or stream to collect freshwater for drinking and cooking.

4 WORLD WATER DAY
China

World Water Day is celebrated all over the world on March 22 each year. Started by the United Nations, the special day focuses on the importance of freshwater conservation and highlights the fact that millions of people around the globe don't have access to clean freshwater. In 2018, as part of a water-saving and antipollution program in Hebei Province, in northeast China, primary school children learned to test for chemicals in water in celebration of World Water Day.

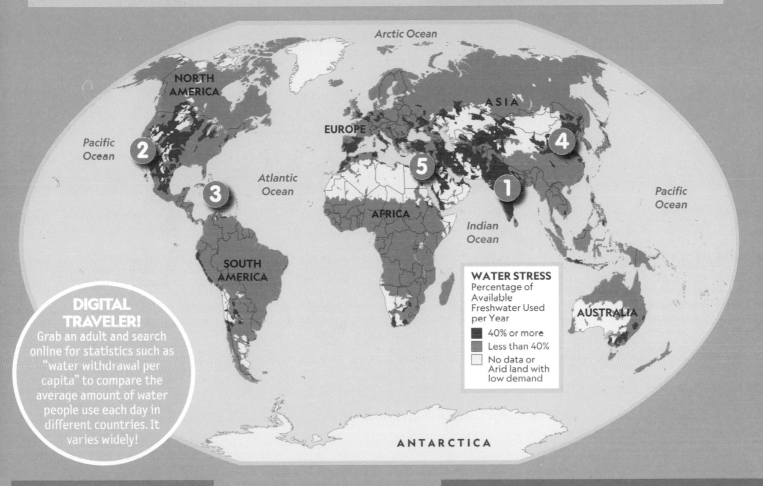

Arctic Ocean

NORTH AMERICA

Pacific Ocean

2

3

Atlantic Ocean

EUROPE

ASIA

4

5

1

AFRICA

Indian Ocean

Pacific Ocean

SOUTH AMERICA

WATER STRESS
Percentage of Available Freshwater Used per Year

- ■ 40% or more
- ■ Less than 40%
- □ No data or Arid land with low demand

AUSTRALIA

ANTARCTICA

DIGITAL TRAVELER!
Grab an adult and search online for statistics such as "water withdrawal per capita" to compare the average amount of water people use each day in different countries. It varies widely!

5 DESALINATION
Gaza Strip

In many countries of the Middle East, where temperatures are high and rainfall low, desalination plants have been set up. Desalination involves removing salt from seawater to produce drinking water. It requires lots of energy, but this can come from renewable solar energy. In Gaza Strip, a desalination plant has helped prevent a water crisis.

TRUE OR FALSE?

Which of these statements about water are true and which are false?

1. The majority of the world's freshwater is used for agriculture.
2. In some parts of the world, people walk an average of three miles (4.8 km) to access a freshwater well.
3. Water is essential for life on Earth.
4. It takes 10 gallons (37.9 L) of water to produce one pound (.45 kg) of plastic.
5. You could be drinking the same water a *T. rex* drank millions of years ago.

FEEDING THE WORLD

See answers on page 150.

5 COOL PROJECTS

1 HELPING POLLINATORS
Japan

The Ginza Honey Bee Project has set up hives atop an office building in the heart of Tokyo, Japan. Its mission is to protect Asian honeybees from population decline and use the insects to pollinate plants. The project is trying to promote sustainable living by using honeybee farming and honey harvesting to produce food within the city.

DIGITAL TRAVELER!

Which country's people eat the most vegetables, meat, dairy products, and seafood? Compare the content of typical diets of peoples from around the world.

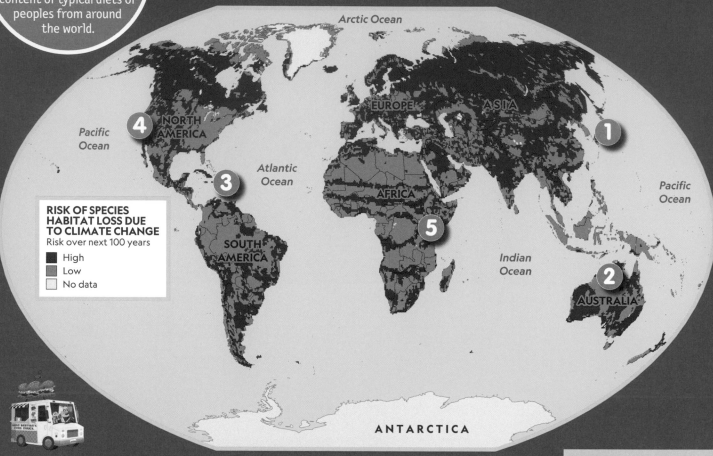

RISK OF SPECIES HABITAT LOSS DUE TO CLIMATE CHANGE
Risk over next 100 years
- ■ High
- ■ Low
- □ No data

2 FOOD BANKS
Australia

As more areas suffer from drought and other natural disasters brought about by climate change, an increasing number of people have trouble accessing fresh food. Combine that with a rise in food prices and even more people go hungry. Food banks throughout the world are helping. Food Bank Australia is a great example. It provided food for more than 77 million meals in 2018.

3 FOOD AID
Puerto Rico

A World Central Kitchen volunteer chef prepares food for people in Puerto Rico following a hurricane in 2017. The food relief organization was founded in 2010 by celebrity chef José Andrés. To date it has provided food services to people in Puerto Rico, Haiti, Zambia, Cambodia, and the continental United States after hurricanes and other natural disasters destroyed communities in these areas.

CLIMATE CHANGE

a soybean crop devastated by drought

THREAT to HABITATS and FOOD SPECIES

As the temperature of Earth's atmosphere rises, habitats—the natural homes of plants and animals—are under threat. Some are becoming drier, hotter, wetter, or windier. Others are regularly flooded or ravaged by firestorms. Rising sea levels threaten coasts and islands. Many plants and animals cannot cope with the changes and are dying out. Familiar crop species, including varieties of strawberries and bananas, and some livestock breeds, no longer thrive in areas where they have been raised for hundreds of years. Many crops are also at risk from the decrease in numbers of insect and bird pollinators that has resulted from habitat change, soil pollution, and the use of pesticides. Without pollinators, many plant foods do not produce fruits and seeds. All of these factors have reduced the amount of food farmers can produce and deliver to food markets and stores. But there are many projects working to overcome these challenges. Here are five cool projects trying to combat the effects of climate change.

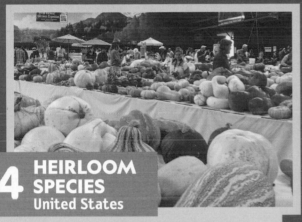

4 HEIRLOOM SPECIES
United States

"Heirloom plants" and "heritage livestock" are crops and farm animal species that have been planted or raised over generations using traditional, natural methods. Because they may need more care, do not grow large, or have unique flavors, the food industry has mostly ignored them. Some farmers are reintroducing these plants and animals to help reduce the use of chemicals and promote sustainable farming and sustainable food consumption. At the annual National Heirloom Expo in California, visitors can sample an abundance of unconventional but delicious food varieties, such as yellow watermelons.

5 FIGHTING HUNGER
Kenya

In many countries around the world, poverty makes it difficult to farm and raise livestock. The organization Heifer International works globally to help poor communities. It provides livestock to farmers and trains them on how to raise and properly care for animals. In Kenya in particular, Heifer International has helped provide goats or cows that produce nutritious milk and meat as well as fertilizer to nourish gardens.

TRUE OR FALSE?

Which of these statements about climate change are true and which are false?

1. Climate change has led to farmers in Vietnam raising seafood on land.
2. A new breed of cattle is helping to combat climate change.
3. Climate change may make it harder for fish to breathe in the ocean.
4. Eating locally grown foods helps fight climate change.
5. In Canada, warmer spring temperatures have increased maple syrup production.

FEEDING THE WORLD

See answers on page 150.

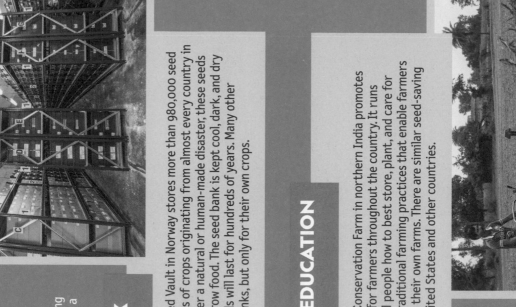

a scientist testing plant samples in a greenhouse

FARMING PRACTICES

LOW- and HI-TECH methods

In less developed countries, farms tend to be small and low-tech. They often follow traditional practices, using animals rather than machinery to work the land. Some have irrigation systems and use chemical fertilizers, while others do not. In more developed countries, farmers can increase their yields by using tractors and other machines. They have access to commercial fertilizers and other chemicals to kill weeds and control pests. They may use high-tech tools, including computers and satellite navigation systems that allow them to plow fields, sow seeds, and spray chemicals at precisely the right location and at the best times of year. Some high-tech farmers grow plants in climate-controlled greenhouses, or grow genetically modified crops that can thrive in difficult conditions. Farmers using such advanced techniques on large commercial farms can produce great quantities of food. But practices that increase yields can also be damaging to the environment. Farmers are constantly challenged to maintain healthy soils, wildlife, and clean water supplies. Here are five projects across the world that are helping both low- and high-tech farmers around the world.

1 SEED BANK
Norway

The Svalbard Global Seed Vault in Norway stores more than 980,000 seed samples, including seeds of crops originating from almost every country in the world. If there is ever a natural or human-made disaster, these seeds can be accessed to regrow food. The seed bank is kept cool, dark, and dry to ensure that the seeds will last for hundreds of years. Many other countries have seed banks, but only for their own crops.

2 FARMING EDUCATION
India

Navdanya Biodiversity Conservation Farm in northern India promotes seed-saving education for farmers throughout the country. It runs programs to teach local people how to best store, plant, and care for seeds. It also teaches traditional farming practices that enable farmers to gain skills needed on their own farms. There are similar seed-saving organizations in the United States and other countries.

3 FOOD AND SOCIETY
Italy

Italy's Slow Food movement is a global program that connects food producers to chefs and food suppliers so that food origins and biodiversity are kept in mind and consumers are given food choices that are healthy for them and the environment. The movement was founded in 1986 to counter the growing fast-food industry.

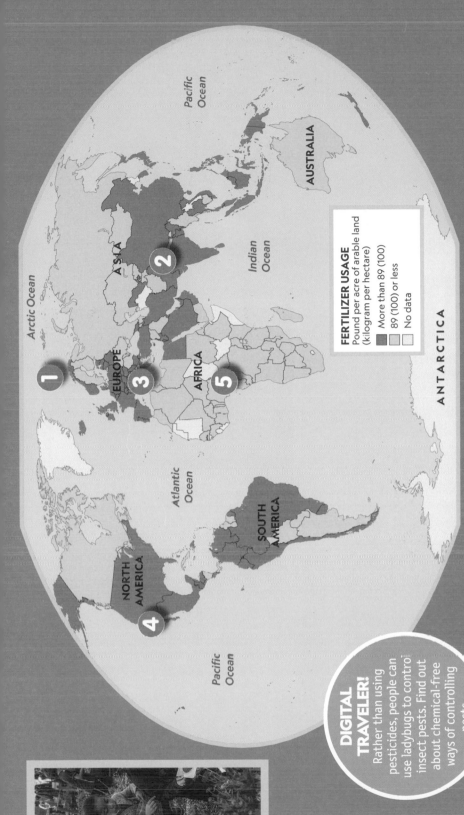

Pacific Ocean

Arctic Ocean

ASIA

② ①

EUROPE ③

Indian Ocean

AUSTRALIA

Pacific Ocean

NORTH AMERICA ④

Atlantic Ocean

AFRICA ⑤

SOUTH AMERICA

ANTARCTICA

FERTILIZER USAGE
Pound per acre of arable land
(kilogram per hectare)
- More than 89 (100)
- 89 (100) or less
- No data

DIGITAL TRAVELER!

Rather than using pesticides, people can use ladybugs to control insect pests. Find out about chemical-free ways of controlling pests.

4 GARDENING FOR KIDS
United States

There is no better place to learn about farming and food than at school. McKinley Elementary School in San Diego, California, has set up a garden where children get hands-on lessons about where their food comes from, how to grow food, and the importance of eating healthy. If your school doesn't have a garden, talk to your teachers about starting one.

TRUE OR FALSE?

Which of these statements about technology used in agriculture are true and which are false?

1. The first gasoline-powered tractor was made in India.
2. Most of the world's food comes from only 12 plant and five animal species.
3. Farmers now use drones to herd cattle.
4. People grew a date palm tree from a seed that was 2,000 years old.
5. There are now robots that can milk cows.

See answers on page 150.

5 CONTROLLING EROSION
Cameroon

Planting trees can help reduce soil erosion and slow climate change. ForestNation is an international organization devoted to tree-planting and raising awareness about the importance of trees. In one Cameroon project, ForestNation helped farmers plant slopes with alternating rows of small trees and legumes, so the trees hold the soil together, while the legumes provide food and enrich the soil.

FOOD SUPPLY

a Vietnamese rice farmer

FACTORS affecting the AVAILABILITY of food

At local, national, and global levels, the food industry tries to match, or balance, the supply and demand for food. That's not easy, because food production isn't always predictable. If conditions are just right, farmers can raise large amounts of crops. But if drought or disease take hold, the harvests suffer. Fishers have good and bad years, too, and overfishing can reduce the amount of fish they catch for years. The workforce can also be an issue. Jobs in the farming and fishing industries involve long, hard hours and low pay. This makes it difficult to attract new employees. And commercial operations are putting small, family-run farms and fisheries out of business, eliminating that option as well. Fortunately, there are projects designed to help people overcome these issues.

5 COOL PROJECTS

1 SMART FOOD SOURCING
Japan

More than ever before, people want to know where their food came from. The World Wide Fund for Nature, known in the United States and Canada as the World Wildlife Fund, is now using digital technology to tag fish caught by fishing vessels in the Pacific Ocean. Once fish are tagged, they can be tracked to supermarkets around the world. This ensures that the seafood is being caught sustainably and prevents illegal, unregulated, and unreported fishing.

2 LOCAL FISHING
Haiti

New fishing boats and fish-processing equipment funded by the organization World Central Kitchen have revitalized the fishing town of Jacmel, Haiti. New fishing boats have enabled the fishers to catch four times the amount that they did in the previous year. And new processing equipment has allowed fishers to get more of their catch to market while it is still fresh.

3 FISH FARMS
Norway

Norway is a world leader in aquaculture—the raising of seafood in artificial enclosures in bodies of salt water or freshwater. Norway's aquaculture farms, located in the country's cool, clear coastal inlets known as fjords, raise foods such as salmon, Norwegian halibut, cod, and prawns. The seafood farms require little energy to operate, so they help combat climate change while also feeding people around the world.

4 CROWDFUNDING FOR FARMERS
Indonesia

The Indonesian crowdfunding platform CROWDE helps small farmers in the country get the funds they need to grow more crops and keep their businesses going. With the help of CROWDE funding, farmers in Sukabumi set up a business growing cucumbers and chili peppers. Others grow onions. This has helped them contribute to and sustain their local food industry.

TRUE OR FALSE?

Which of these statements about food are true and which are false?

1. The United States has the second largest fishing industry in the world.
2. The average dairy cow produces two gallons (7.6 L) of milk per day.
3. There are three breeds of sheep in Canada.
4. The three crops we rely on most for food are rice, wheat, and corn.
5. The plastics we throw away can end up in the food we eat.

See answers on page 150.

ARCTIC OCEAN

North America — ③ Europe — Asia — ①

PACIFIC OCEAN

ATLANTIC OCEAN — ②

Africa

■ Areas where fewer fish are being caught*

*Not all fish species shown

South America

INDIAN OCEAN — ④

PACIFIC OCEAN

Australia

Antarctica

DIGITAL TRAVELER!

Globally, China is the largest producer of fish, accounting for about one third of all catches. Find the main species of fish it harvests from the seas and raises on farms.

5 GROWING FARMERS
United States

The Growing Farmers Initiative at the Stone Barns Center for Food & Agriculture in New York State offers apprenticeship programs that teach young farmers how to operate and run their own farms. It also promotes community-based food production. Crops and animals raised on the center's farm using sustainable agriculture practices are prepared and served at the Stone Barns Center's restaurant.

FEEDING THE WORLD

COLOR CODED

Some items on this Hawaiian beach have mysteriously changed color. Find 12 things that are the wrong color.

ANSWERS ON PAGE 151

FRESH FRUIT FOR SALE

WHAT IN THE WORLD?

FLAG FRENZY

These photos show close-up views of flags from countries around the world. Unscramble the letters to identify which country's flag is shown in each picture. Bonus: Use the highlighted letters to solve the puzzle below.

ANSWERS ON PAGE 151

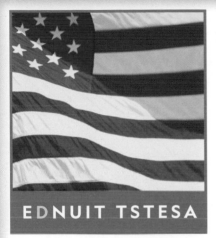

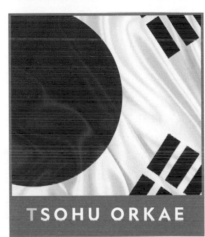

EDNUIT TSTESA

ARZBLI

YNAOWR

DIINA

TSOHU ORKAE

LIARAGE

EERECG

HUOTS FACRAI

IPASN

HINT: Why did the flag need to rest?

ANSWER: __ __O_ _____.

145

WHAT IN THE WORLD?

JUNGLE GOODS

These photos show close-up views of items that come from rainforest plants. Unscramble the letters to identify what's in each picture. Bonus: Use the highlighted letters to solve the puzzle below.

ANSWERS ON PAGE 151

NASAANB

OREP

OFEFEC

NOICANMN

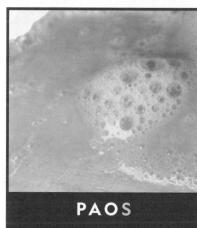

PAOS

LCOOTHAEC

IEHNWCG MGU

BRUEBR RTISE

ZLIARB TNSU

HINT: What did the toucan say to the cashier?

ANSWER: J _ _ _   _ _ T _ _   _ N _ Y _ _ _ _ !

READY, SET, EAT!

These neighbors have gathered for a Thanksgiving potluck dinner, but all the food has gone missing from the kitchen. Find the 15 items on the list so the guests can enjoy their meal.

1. baked potato
2. green beans
3. roast turkey
4. carrots
5. pumpkin pie
6. cauliflower
7. mushrooms
8. cranberry sauce
9. gravy
10. corn
11. apple
12. baguette
13. brussels sprouts
14. bell peppers
15. asparagus

ANSWERS ON PAGE 151

MARKET MIX-UP

The Damnoen Saduak Floating Market in Thailand is filled with amazing goods. But 15 of the items are in the wrong place. Find each number, figure out what's missing, and search the picture to find it. For example, number 1 shows a missing postcard, which has been misplaced on a boat.

ANSWERS ON PAGE 151

ANSWERS

28: True or False?

1. True
2. False. Corn is fed mainly to livestock.
3. False. Corn mazes are an attraction in the fall.
4. True. Chicha morada is a soft drink made from purple maize.
5. False—sure it is! Some species of corn are grown specifically to be sold as popping corns.

48: True or False?

1. True. Fair trade offers farmers a good market price for their crops.
2. True. Chemicals in chocolate give them an upset stomach.
3. False. Chocolate melts at about 10°F (5.6°C) lower than a human body temperature of 98.6°F (37°C).
4. False. It was first made by the Olmec people of Central America about 3,000 years ago.
5. True

68: True or False?

1. True
2. False. It takes about 10 pounds (4.5 kg) of cow's or goat's milk, or 6 pounds (2.7 kg) of sheep's milk, to make a pound (.45 kg) of cheese.
3. True
4. True
5. False. Chinese people eat less cheese than anyone else.

89: True or False?

1. True
2. False. Sugar is naturally white.
3. True
4. True. Maple syrup and honey both contain fructose.
5. True

108: True or False?

1. True
2. True
3. False. Spices come from a plant's bark, buds, stem, roots, bulb, seeds, or fruits. Herbs come from the leaves.

4. False. It is the national spice of Hungary. Guatemala does not have a national spice.
5. True. This test is known as the Scoville scale.

129: True or False?

1. False. It's good for cooking and your skin but it's not good for your bike.
2. True. Pig-tailed macaques are specially trained to harvest coconuts.
3. True. In botany this type of fruit is called a drupe.
4. False. The milk is made by mixing shredded coconut flesh with water, heating it, and straining out the liquid.
5. True

137: True or False?

1. True. About 70 percent is used for agriculture.
2. True. Many people in Africa must walk an average of three miles (4.8 km) to fill buckets with water and then return home with full buckets.
3. True. For example, without water, a person can live for only three or four days.
4. False. It takes about 22 gallons (83.3 L) of water to produce a pound (.45 kg) of plastic.
5. True. The same water has moved and changed from one form to another over millions of years in Earth's water cycle.

139: Answers: True or False?

1. True. They use aquaculture in former rice fields.
2. True. The cattle pass less methane gas.
3. True. Ocean waters are more acidic because of climate change. It's harder for fish to get oxygen to breathe out of acidic waters.
4. True. Shorter delivery trips mean fewer emissions are released into the environment.

5. False. The season for collecting sap from the trees has shortened in the past 50 years.

141: Answers: True or False?

1. False. It was made in Iowa, U.S.A., in 1892.
2. True. Seventy-five percent of the foods we eat come from these 17 species. This lack of diversity opens us up to problems if any of these species should fail.
3. True
4. True. The seed was found during an archaeological dig and then germinated in a laboratory. However, most seeds have a lifespan of less than 10 years.
5. True

143: Answers: True or False?

1. False. It is India. The United States has the fifth largest fishing industry in the world.
2. False. Dairy cows produce about seven gallons (26.5 L) of milk per day.
3. False. There are more than 50 breeds of sheep in Canada (and the United States).
4. True
5. True. In oceans, plastic waste breaks down into tiny particles. These are taken in by ocean wildlife and enter the food chain. When we eat fish and shellfish that have consumed the tiny particles, these microplastics end up in our bodies.

AUNT BERTHA
Aunt Bertha appears inside the pages of this book 33 times. She's also on the cover 8 times.

144: Color Coded

145: What in the World?
Top row: United States, Brazil, Norway
Middle row: India, South Korea, Algeria
Bottom row: Greece, South Africa, Spain
Bonus: It got winded.

146: What in the World?
Top row: bananas, rope, coffee
Middle row: cinnamon, soap, chocolate
Bottom row: chewing gum, rubber tires,
   Brazil nuts
Bonus: Just put it on my bill!

147: Ready, Set, Eat!

148–149: Market Mix-Up

GLOSSARY

Use this glossary of foods, cooking, and geographic terms to help you find dishes, drinks, and recipes all over the world.

agriculture another term for farming

appetizer a small dish or bite of food that is eaten before the main course, or entrée

aquaculture the farming of fish, shellfish, or other foods from freshwater or saltwater

bake to cook in an oven without an open flame

barbecue a meal of foods cooked over an open fire; to grill outdoors

batter a thin, whisked or beaten dough used to coat fried foods or to make pancakes, cakes, and other foods

beat to mix by rapidly stirring

blend to combine two or more ingredients until they are smooth; a smooth mixture of two or more ingredients

boil to heat a liquid, such as water, until it begins to vaporize and bubble

breed a form of a species selected and raised by farmers for food; to produce offspring

broil to cook by exposure to direct heat, one side at a time

broth a savory liquid often used in making soups

bulb a swollen, underground, modified stem with fleshy leaves or leaf bases that stores food for a plant. A new plant can grow from a bulb.

burrito a Mexican dish consisting of a flour tortilla filled with items such as meat, cheese, and beans

caramelize to cook something, such as a fruit or vegetable, until it becomes brown and sweet

carnitas a Mexican dish of simmered pork

casserole a dish of meat, vegetables, or other foods cooked slowly at a low temperature in a deep dish

cereals plants of the grass family that produce small edible seeds, including corn, wheat, barley, oats, and rice

chapulines a Mexican dish of cooked grasshoppers

chop to cut into bite-size pieces; a cut of meat attached to a rib

clamming digging for clams on a sandy beach

coat to apply a layer of something, as in strawberries coated with chocolate

cob the large fruit of corn plants that bears a mass of kernels

continent one of the seven main landmasses on Earth's surface

corn a small cereal grain, also known as maize

cornmeal a coarse, sandy flour made from ground dried corn

cream to beat something into a creamy froth; a thick milk product with a high fat content

cultivate to prepare and use land for growing crops

cure a process of food preservation that draws out moisture

cut in to mix a solid fat, such as butter, into flour using a pastry blender until evenly distributed

dairy foods produced from the milk of mammals, including cows, goats, sheep, camels, and buffalo

deep fry to cook something by submerging it in hot oil or fat

dice to cut food into tiny, uniform pieces

dim sum Chinese bite-size dishes served on small plates or in steamer baskets

dish a flat food container, or the food served on it; a particular food prepared as part of a meal

dissolve when a solid becomes part of a liquid, forming a solution

dollop a small, round amount of a food item such as whipped cream that is served as part of a dish

dolma Mediterranean prepared food of leaves— usually cabbage—rolled and stuffed with a filling of meat, rice, or herbs

drizzle to pour a thin stream of liquid over food

dust to sprinkle sugar, flour, or another substance on something

eggplant a smooth, deep purple fruit also known as an aubergine

environment the conditions surrounding and affecting any living thing, including the climate, landscape, and other living things

erosion the wearing away of land due to water, wind, rain, or snow

fair trade a system of trading in which producers are paid a fair price, have decent working conditions, and promote sustainable practices

ferment to break down the sugars in a food through a chemical reaction

fertilizer a chemical used to increase plant growth

feta a crumbly cheese made from goat's or sheep's milk, popular in Greece

fjord a deep, narrow sea inlet surrounded by high cliffs

fold to carefully combine two ingredients of different consistencies, such as whipped cream in cake batter; to wrap around itself

fondue a dish in which small pieces of food, like meat or fruit, are dipped in a hot liquid to cook before eating

fritter a fried food such as a vegetable or seafood cooked in a batter

fruit the often sweet and fleshy seed-containing product of a flowering plant; includes nuts, berries, and pods

fry to cook food in hot oil or fat

fungi a group of organisms, including mushrooms and toadstools, that break down and absorb other once living organisms

gelato Italian-style ice cream made with milk, little cream, and sometimes without eggs

genetically modified food produced from plants or animals whose DNA has been modified through genetic engineering

ghee clarified butter used in Indian cooking

glaze to coat food with a sweet, glossy material such as honey

grain a small edible seed of a cereal crop

grate to reduce a food such as cheese to shreds by scraping it against a rough surface

gratin a food dish topped with bread crumbs or cheese

grill a metal frame used in outdoor cooking over an open flame; to cook food under or over an open flame

grind to reduce a spice or other food to a powder

gumbo a stew made with okra and greens in the French West Indies and Louisiana

heirloom an old variety of flower, fruit, or vegetable

herb a plant used for flavoring, food, medicine, or perfume

indigenous not brought from somewhere else; originally grown or living in a country or region

ingredients items used to create a food dish

kefir a fermented milk drink

knead to fold and squeeze dough

legume a plant that produces pods containing peas, beans, or lentils

livestock farm animals such as cows, horses, goats, and pigs that are kept for their meat, milk, and other products

macerate to soften by putting in liquid, often used to make meat tender

maize an American cereal plant, often called corn

marinate to soak meat or other food in a liquid for flavor

Middle East a term commonly used for the countries of southwestern Asia, including Kuwait, Iran, Iraq, United Arab Emirates, Syria, Lebanon, Israel, Egypt, and Jordan

mince food ground up into tiny bits, or the grinding process itself

mix to combine items together

mole a traditional Mexican sauce that often includes chocolate

mousse a smooth, pudding-like dish that can be served as a sweet dessert or a savory dish

mozzarella white, mild-tasting soft Italian cheese traditionally made from buffalo's milk

native born in or originating from a particular place

noodles long, thin strips of pasta or another flour paste served in a sauce or soup

Northern Hemisphere the half of the globe that lies north of the Equator. It includes all of North America, a small part of South America, all of Europe, about two-thirds of Africa, and almost all of Asia.

nutrient a chemical or compound in food needed for growth. Plant nutrients include nitrogen, potassium, and phosphorus. Animal nutrients include proteins, fats, carbohydrates, and vitamins.

oil in cooking, a liquid vegetable product used to fry food or, as in olive oil, as a dressing for salads

organic farming producing food using only natural fertilizers and pesticides

Pampas the flat, treeless part of southern South America between the Atlantic coast and the Andes mountains. It has many cattle ranches.

pasta an Italian dish made of durum or semolina wheat that is served in a variety of shapes and sizes

pastry a type of dessert made of baked dough filled with cream, jam, or other sweet mixture, or a crust of the baked dough itself

peel to remove the outer covering of a vegetable or fruit, or the outer covering of a vegetable or fruit itself

pesticide a substance that kills any pest, including insects, fungi, and weeds

pesto a sauce of crushed herbs, such as basil, along with pine nuts and olive oil

pickle to preserve in vinegar; a cucumber or other vegetable or fruit that has been pickled

pinch the amount of a substance you can hold between your thumb and forefinger

plain a large area of relatively flat land

plantation a large farm or estate that uses lots of people to raise and harvest crops such as apples

poach to cook by simmering in a small amount of water or other liquid

pork meat of a pig used for food

poultry meat of a chicken or other bird used for food

pudding a creamy dessert or an English steamed dish

puree a food that is pressed or blended into a creamy consistency

quiche an unsweetened custard-like mixture of eggs, milk, or cream filled with meat, fish, or vegetables

rainforest a dense forest that gets a heavy amount of rainfall, usually found near the Equator

ranch a large farm where livestock is raised

rhizome a swollen, underground, modified stem that sends out roots and shoots and stores food for a plant. A new plant can grow from a rhizome.

roast to use dry heat to cook meat or vegetables

root crop a crop such as carrots, turnips, or parsnips that is grown for its enlarged edible roots

savanna a tropical grassland with scattered trees

seafood edible fish, seaweed, or shellfish from the sea

season to add a flavoring, such as salt or spices, to a food; part of a year with distinct weather

seaweed a type of algae; sea plants or sea vegetables growing in the ocean and eaten in many forms

shellfish mollusks, crustaceans, and echinoderms, such as clams, shrimps, and sea urchins

shred to cut or tear food into thin strips

simmer to slowly cook in a liquid below the boiling point

skewer a shaft of metal or wood that vegetables and meats are fastened to as they are broiled or grilled

skim to remove a layer of scum or impurities from a cooking liquid

skyr an Icelandic dairy product similar to a mild-tasting yogurt

Southern Hemisphere the half of the globe that lies south of the Equator. It includes most of South America, a third of Africa, all of Australia and Oceania, all of Antarctica, and a small part of Asia

species a class of living things that have the same characteristics and share a common scientific name

spice a plant seed, bark, stem, or root used for seasoning food

staple a chief component of people's diet

steam vapor that rises from boiling water and can be used to cook food

steppe relatively flat, mostly treeless grassland that stretches across much of southeastern Europe and Central Asia

sticky rice a variety of rice that requires less water in preparation and sticks together when cooked

street food ready-to-eat food that is sold by vendors on the street rather than in restaurants

stew to boil slowly with simmering heat; a soup-like mixture of meat and vegetables that is cooked slowly

stir to mix foods in a circular motion, usually with a spoon

stir-fry an Asian cooking method that often uses a wok to fry bite-size fresh vegetables and meats in a light oil

sushi traditional Japanese dish made from seasoned rice, seaweed, vegetables, and/or assorted raw fish

sustainable produced and harvested in a way that does not overuse resources or stocks or harm the environment

tagine an earthenware dish used for cooking that originated in Morocco

tahini a flavorful paste made from sesame seeds, used in Mediterranean dishes

tart a small pastry or pie with no top that is filled with jams, custard, or jellies; a sharp flavor

tofu a food produced from pressed soy milk, often called bean curd

tortilla round, thin cornmeal or wheat unleavened bread served with an assortment of toppings or fillings

tropical from the region of Earth lying within about 23° north and south of the Equator that experiences warm temperatures year-round

truffle a type of edible fungus that grows below ground

tuber a swollen, underground plant stem or side root used as food; potatoes and yams are stem tubers, sweet potatoes and cassavas are root tubers

variety one of many different types of plants or animals

vegetable a plant or part of a plant used for food, such as a carrot, beet, or lettuce

waffle a crisp breakfast food made from batter cooked between two heated plates

whip to vigorously beat foods like cream or eggs into a froth, using a utensil such as a whisk

whisk a cooking utensil with many loops of wire that is used to whip foods

yogurt a dairy food made from bacterial fermentation and eaten plain or with fruit or used as an ingredient in recipes

zest the finely grated peel of citrus fruits, used to add flavor to recipes

tropical fruits

INDEX

PHOTO CREDITS

Abbreviations: AL=Alamy Stock Photo; DRMS=Dreamstime; GI=Getty Images; SS=Shutterstock

Front cover: (spaghetti & meatballs), Marysckin/SS; (food trucks), BluIz60/AL; (plantains), Ildi Papp/SS; (legumes), Andrii Gorulko/SS; (empanadas), bhofack2/iStockphoto/GI; (cheeseburger), gresei/SS; (farm), maksymowicz/Adobe Stock; (sushi), joesayhello/SS

Back cover: (café), Iakov Filimonov/SS; (cheeses), Nikolay Dimitrov/SS; (farm truck), salmon-negro/SS

Front matter: 2 (LO LE), Ppy2010ha/DRMS; 2 (CTR), Rodrigo De Souza Mendes Junqueira/DRMS; 2 (LO RT), Nadianb/DRMS; 3 (UP LE), Artitwpd/DRMS; 3 (UP RT), Sandy Huffaker/Corbis/GI; 3 (CTR), Bhofack2/DRMS; 3 (LO), Alexander Mychko/DRMS; 6 (UP), 7xpert/DRMS

North America: 10 (LO), Jon Bilous/DRMS; 12 (UP), LianeM/SS; 12 (LO), Larisa Blinova/SS; 13 (UP), Elena Elisseeva/DRMS; 13 (CTR), Rachel Moon/SS; 13 (LO LE), Pamela Mcadams/DRMS; 13 (LO RT), Hans Geel/DRMS; 14 (UP), Manyakotic/DRMS; 14 (CTR), Afed4enko/DRMS; 14 (LO), Alexander Mychko/DRMS; 15 (UP), Marazem/DRMS; 15 (CTR), Nancy F. Castaldo; 15 (LO), Billion Photos/SS; 16 (UP RT), Alp Aksoy/DRMS; 16 (LO LE), Nevinates/DRMS; 16 (LO RT), Susabell/DRMS; 17 (UP RT), Alexander Mychko/DRMS; 17 (LO LE), Svetlana Foote/DRMS; 17 (LO RT), Sergii Koval/DRMS; 18 (UP), Prisma by Dukas Presseagentur GmbH/AL; 18 (CTR), Leigh Anne Meeks/DRMS; 18 (LO LE), Oksanabratanova/DRMS; 18 (LO RT), Mike Clegg/DRMS; 19 (UP), dbimages/AL; 19 (LO), Philip Scalia/AL; 20 (UP), bbivirys/Adobe Stock; 20 (CTR), Ppy2010ha/DRMS; 20 (LO), DronG/SS; 21 (UP), canada/AL; 21 (CTR), Han Van Vonno/DRMS; 21 (LO), Antonio Gravante/AL; 22 (UP LE), Robert Lerich/DRMS; 22 (UP RT), Natashaphoto/DRMS; 22 (LO), Triciadaniel/DRMS; 23 (CTR), Vasiliy Budarin/DRMS; 23 (UP), Photomailbox/DRMS; 24 (CTR), Homydesign/DRMS; 23 (LO), Ppy2010ha/DRMS; 24 (UP), DronG/SS; 24 (CTR), Homydesign/DRMS; 24 (LO LE), Annapustynnikova/DRMS; 24 (LO RT), Leigh Beisch/StockFood; 25 (UP), Mantoniuk/DRMS; 25 (LO), Etiennevoss/DRMS; 26 (LE), vsl/SS; 26 (RT), Diavolica/DRMS; 27 (UP LE), Bhofack2/DRMS; 27 (UP RT), PatChan_HK/SS; 27 (CTR), Bhofack2/DRMS; 27 (LO), Cao Hai/DRMS; 28 (UP), Marcos Castillo/DRMS; 28 (LO), JerryDeutsch/SS; 29 (UP), Kuhar/DRMS; 29 (CTR LE), Tatsiana Hendzel/DRMS; 29 (CTR RT), Gaurav Masand/DRMS; 29 (LO), Iuliia Timofeeva/DRMS

South America: 30 (LO), Nika Lerman/DRMS; 32 (UP), Edgloris Marys/DRMS; 32 (LO), Laurange Unbekandt/AL; 33 (UP), Vinicius Tupinamba/DRMS; 33 (CTR RT), Vanilla/DRMS; 33 (CTR LE), Diogo Piloto Proenca/DRMS; 33 (LO), Damian Olivera Bergallo/DRMS; 34 (UP LE), Alexander Mychko/DRMS; 34 (UP RT), Oliver Foerstner/DRMS; 34 (LO), Alexander Mychko/DRMS; 35 (UP), Larisa Blinova/DRMS; 35 (CTR), Kondratova/DRMS; 35 (LO), Nicholas Gill/AL; 36 (UP), Stephan Bock/DRMS; 36 (CTR), Eq Roy/DRMS; 36 (LO), Ppy2010ha/DRMS; 37 (UP), Alexander Mychko/DRMS; 37 (LO LE), Betta0147/DRMS; 37 (LO RT), Gkmf10/DRMS; 38 (UP LE), robertharding/AL; 38 (UP RT), David R. Frazier Photolibrary, Inc./AL; 38 (LO), Vespasian/AL; 39 (UP), Patricio Realpe/GI; 39 (LO LE), Luiz Ribeiro/DRMS; 39 (LO RT), Ernesto Benavides/AFP/GI; 40 (UP), SuperStock/AL; 40 (CTR), Ppy2010ha/DRMS; 40 (LO), Prisma by Dukas Presseagentur GmbH/AL; 41 (UP), Ppy2010ha/DRMS; 41 (LO LE), Raluca Tudor/DRMS; 41 (LO RT), Ian Trower/robertharding.com; 42 (UP), Ildipapp/DRMS; 42 (LO LE), Ildipapp/DRMS; 42 (LO RT), Rafael Ben Ari/DRMS; 42-43 (UP), Carlos Soler Martinez/DRMS; 43 (CTR), Tycoon751/DRMS; 44 (UP LE), Brizardh/DRMS; 44 (UP RT), Marco Ramerini/DRMS; 44 (LO), Iuliia Timofeeva/DRMS; 45 (UP), Matyas Rehak/DRMS; 45 (LO LE), Julie Feinstein/DRMS; 45 (LO RT), Rodrigo De Souza Mendes Junqueira/DRMS; 46 (UP), Presse750/DRMS; 46 (CTR), Pablo Hidalgo/DRMS; 46 (LO), robertharding/AL; 47 (UP LE), Mark Green/AL; 47 (UP RT), Larisa Blinova/AL; 47 (LO), Petroos/DRMS; 48 (UP), Adisa/DRMS; 48 (CTR), oddziie/SS; 48 (LO), anna quaglia/AL; 49 (UP LE), Dolphy/DRMS; 49 (UP RT), Leithan Partnership t/a The Picture Pantry/AL; 49 (LO), Sia Kambou/AFP/GI

Europe: 50 (LO), Roman Davydov/DRMS; 52 (UP), Jenny Tonkin Nature images/AL; 52 (CTR), Roman Milert/DRMS; 52 (LO), Inga Nielsen/DRMS; 53 (UP), Bombaert/DRMS; 53 (LO LE), Yuliakotina/DRMS; 53 (LO RT), Bhofack2/DRMS; 54 (UP), Kati Kemppainen/DRMS; 54 (CTR), Ksena2009/DRMS; 54 (LO), Bruno Rosa/DRMS; 55 (UP), Freeskyline/DRMS; 55 (LO LE), Canadapanda/DRMS; 55 (LO RT), Kabvisio/DRMS; 56 (UP LE), Andrey Semenov/DRMS; 56 (UP RT), Ewa Rejmer/DRMS; 56 (LO LE), Marilyn Barbone/DRMS; 56-57 (UP), Alexander Mychko/DRMS; 57 (UP RT), Ginasanders/DRMS; 57 (CTR), Ppy2010ha/DRMS; 57 (LO), Yurakp/DRMS; 58 (UP), Denise Serra/DRMS; 58 (LO LE), Danil Snigirev/DRMS; 58 (LO RT), Artur Widak/NurPhoto/GI; 59 (UP RT), Anke Van Wyk/DRMS; 59 (CTR LE), Mattiass/DRMS; 59 (LO), Fabrice Coffrini/AFP/GI; 60 (UP), stockcreations/DRMS; 60 (CTR), ULD photo life/SS; 60 (LO), Fabrizia Postiglione/StockFood; 61 (UP), 18042011e/DRMS; 61 (LO), imageBROKER/AL; 62 (UP), Alexander Mychko/DRMS; 62 (CTR), Ezumeimages/DRMS; 63 (UP), Sergii Koval/DRMS; 63 (LO LE), Rawdon Wyatt/StockFood; 63 (LO RT), Alexander Mychko/DRMS; 64 (UP LE), Imagestore/DRMS; 64 (CTR), stockcreations/DRMS; 64 (LO), Doupix/DRMS; 64-65 (LO), Sabine Löscher/StockFood; 65 (UP RT), Photomailbox/DRMS; 65 (LO), Fedecandoniphoto/DRMS; 66 (UP LE), Monty Rakusen/GI; 66 (CTR), Kudryavtsev/DRMS; 66 (LO), Artem Mokrietsov/DRMS; 66-67 (UP), Joseph Gough/DRMS; 67 (LO LE), Ppy2010ha/DRMS; 67 (LO RT), Great Stock!/StockFood; 68 (UP), Alexandr Kornienko/DRMS; 68 (CTR), stockcreations/DRMS; 68 (LO), Tatiane Silva/SS; 69 (UP), AS Food studio/SS; 69 (LO LE), Stock Image Factory/DRMS; 69 (LO RT), NaturalBox/SS

Asia: 70 (LO), Kalcutta/DRMS; 72 (UP), Magdanatka/SS; 72 (LO LE), Sergey Rusanov/DRMS; 72 (LO RT), Methinee Chairangsinan/DRMS; 73 (UP), Mikhail Dudarev/DRMS; 73 (LO LE), Ppy2010ha/DRMS; 73 (LO RT), Vadim Zakirov/DRMS; 74 (UP), Artitwpd/DRMS; 74 (LO LE), Plmrue/DRMS; 74 (LO RT), Feroze/DRMS; 75 (UP), Numpon Jumroonsiri/DRMS; 75 (CTR), Gayane/DRMS; 75 (LO), Evgeniy Fesenko/DRMS; 76 (UP), Szefei/DRMS; 76 (CTR LE), Ursula Schersch/StockFood; 76 (CTR RT), Vojtaler/out.com/DRMS; 77 (UP LE), Nevinates/DRMS; 77 (UP RT), Shutterbestiole/DRMS; 78 (UP), Dinodia Photos/AL; 78 (CTR LE), Eddie Gerald/AL; 78 (CTR RT), Minadezhda/DRMS; 78-79 (LO), Robinson Thomas/AL; 79 (UP), Gina Ferazzi/Los Angeles Times/GI; 79 (LO), Sin See Ho/AL; 80 (UP LE), Phichak Limprasutr/DRMS; 80 (CTR), bonchan/SS; 80 (LO), Evgeniy Fesenko/DRMS; 80-81 (UP), Natalia Zakharova/DRMS; 81 (UP RT), norikko/SS; 81 (LO), Alexander Mychko/DRMS; 82 (UP LE), Ppy2010ha/DRMS; 82 (UP RT), Pongsak Tiantad/DRMS; 82 (CTR), Ppy2010ha/DRMS; 82-83 (LO), Alexander Mychko/DRMS; 83 (UP), travelib asia/AL; 83 (LO RT), Tim Whitby/AL; 84 (UP LE), Seersa Abaza/AL; 84 (UP RT), zkruger/SS; 84 (LO LE), Vladimir Konstantinov/SS; 84-85 (LO), Edmensis/SS; 85 (UP), Gunold/DRMS; 85 (CTR), Hein Teh/DRMS; 86 (UP), Ultraone/DRMS; 86 (CTR), john wreford/AL; 86 (LO), Keechuan/DRMS; 87 (UP), Anujavijay/DRMS; 87 (CTR), Petr Goskov/DRMS; 87 (LO), Valya82/DRMS; 88 (CTR), Elena Schweitzer/SS; 88 (CTR), Bhofack2/DRMS; 88 (LO), Prudencio Alvarez/DRMS; 89 (UP LE), Joanna Dorota/SS; 89 (UP RT), Andrea Magugliani/AL; 89 (LO), Etcheverry Collection/AL

Africa: 90 (LO), Georg Berg/AL; 92 (UP), Sjors737/DRMS; 92 (CTR), Pipa100/DRMS; 92-93 (LO), Joerg Boethling/AL; 93 (UP), Cristina Dini/DRMS; 93 (CTR), Tatyana Aksenova/DRMS; 93 (LO), Somchai Rak-in/DRMS; 94 (UP), Kewuwu/DRMS; 94 (CTR), Joan Egert/DRMS; 94 (LO), Alexander Mychko/DRMS; 95 (UP LE), Mujib Waziri/DRMS; 95 (UP RT), Afripics/AL; 95 (CTR), Nipaporn Panyacharoen/DRMS; 96 (UP LE), David Buzzard/AL; 96 (UP RT), Alexander Mychko/DRMS; 96 (LO), Alexander Mychko/DRMS; 97 (UP), Jianghongyan/DRMS; 97 (CTR), Alexander Mychko/DRMS; 97 (LO), Matthew Omojola/DRMS; 98 (UP), Adou Innocent Kouadio/DRMS; 98 (CTR), Isaac Kasamani/AFP/GI; 98 (LO), Jerónimo Alba/AL; 99 (CTR), Ryad Kramdi/AFP/GI; 99 (LO), dbimages/AL; 100 (UP LE), Boonchuay Iamsumang/DRMS; 100 (UP RT), Simon Reddy/AL; 100 (LO), A1977/DRMS; 101 (LO LE), Alexander Mychko/DRMS; 101 (LO CTR), Txarofranco/DRMS; 101 (LO RT), Largonadya/DRMS; 102 (UP), Edward Westmacott/DRMS; 102 (CTR LE), Vladlena Azima/DRMS; 102 (CTR RT), Alexander Mychko/DRMS; 102 (LO), Simon Reddy/AL; 103 (UP), Abraham Badenhorst/DRMS; 103 (LO), Edwin Remsburg/VW Pics/GI; 104 (UP), Marwan Naamani/AFP/GI; 104 (CTR), Simon Reddy/AL; 104 (LO LE), Fadel Senna/AFP/GI; 104 (LO RT), Georges Gobet/AFP/GI; 105 (UP LE), Bartosz Luczak/DRMS; 105 (UP RT), Alexander Mychko/DRMS; 106 (UP), Danita Delimont/AL; 106 (CTR), lhmfoto/SS; 106 (LO), Cultura Creative (RF)/AL; 107 (UP), Edwardgerges/DRMS; 107 (LO LE), Universal Images Group North America LLC/DeAgostini/AL; 107 (LO RT), Education Images/Universal Images Group/GI; 108 (UP), Lubos Chlubny/DRMS; 108 (LO LE), Ksk1977/DRMS; 108 (LO RT), Teubner Foodfoto/StockFood; 109 (UP), Robyn Mackenzie/DRMS; 109 (LO LE), foodfolio/AL; 109 (LO RT), Joseph Gough/DRMS

Australia and Oceania: 110 (LO), Michal Knitl/SS; 112 (UP), Msphotographic/DRMS; 112 (CTR), 2p2play/SS; 112 (LO), Setiko/DRMS; 113 (UP), Pixinoo/DRMS; 113 (CTR), Johnfoto/DRMS; 113 (LO), Baronb/SS; 114 (UP LE), Edd Westmacott/AL; 114 (UP RT), Alexander Mychko/DRMS; 114 (LO LE), Hilde Mèche/StockFood; 114 (LO RT), CKP1001/SS; 115 (UP), Laszlo Konya/DRMS; 115 (CTR), Bhofack2/DRMS; 115 (LO), Antonio Magdaraog/DRMS; 116 (UP), Valentina Razumova/DRMS; 116 (CTR), Nipaporn Panyacharoen/DRMS; 116 (LO), Yardpirun Saengtong/DRMS; 117 (UP), Brightcolors0412/DRMS; 117 (CTR), Eising Studio - Food Photo & Video/StockFood; 117 (LO), raksyBH/DRMS; 118 (UP), Eric Lafforgue/Gamma-Rapho/GI; 118 (CTR), Ross Henry/DRMS; 118 (LO LE), FLX2/SS; 118 (LO RT), Kai Schwoerer/GI; 119 (UP), Glenn Martin/DRMS; 119 (LO LE), Rafael Ben Ari/DRMS; 119 (LO RT), Keren Su/China Span/AL; 120 (UP), Margo555/DRMS; 120 (CTR), Robyn Mackenzie/DRMS; 120 (LO), vm2002/SS; 121 (UP LE), Marek Uliasz/DRMS; 121 (UP RT), Victor Diola Jr/DRMS; 121 (LO), Saletomic/DRMS; 122 (UP), Byelikova/DRMS; 122 (LO LE), John Kelly/AL; 122 (LO RT), Leigh Anne Meeks/DRMS; 123 (UP), Avalon/Photoshot License/AL; 123 (CTR), stockcreations/DRMS; 123 (LO), Alexander Mychko/DRMS; 124 (UP), Janet Hastings/DRMS; 124 (CTR), Laurange/StockFood; 124 (LO), Ymgerman/DRMS; 125 (UP LE), IgorGolovniov/SS; 125 (UP RT), Sheryl Caston/DRMS; 125 (CTR), Dorling Kindersley ltd/AL; 126 (UP LE), AusAID/AL; 126 (UP RT), Zkruger/DRMS; 126 (LO), Rafael Ben Ari/DRMS; 127 (CTR), Cornelia Luethi/AL; 127 (LO LE), Sourcenext/AL; 127 (LO RT), Alexander Mychko/DRMS; 128 (UP LE), Bert Folsom/DRMS; 128 (UP RT), Paul Brighton/DRMS; 128 (LO), Jikung4u/DRMS; 129 (UP), Sayompoo/DRMS; 129 (CTR), Andre Baranowski/StockFood; 129 (LO), Mypointofview/DRMS

Oceans: 132 (UP), Hans-Joachim Aubert/AL; 132 (CTR), Claudio Monni/DRMS; 132 (LO), Colin Erricson/StockFood; 133 (UP), Gräfe & Unzer Verlag/Kramp + Gölling/StockFood; 133 (LO LE), Biosphoto/AL; 133 (LO RT), Alexander Mychko/DRMS

Feeding the World: 136 (UP LE), Jake Lyell/AL; 136 (UP RT), Education Images/Universal Images Group/GI; 136 (LO LE), Dinodia Photos/AL; 136 (LO RT), Thomas Lohnes/GI; 137 (UP), SIPA Asia via ZUMA Wire/AL; 137 (LO), Said Khatib/AFP/GI; 138 (UP), Chris McGrath/GI; 138 (LO LE), Xinhua/AL; 138 (LO RT), AB Forces News Collection/AL; 139 (UP), USDA Photo/AL; 139 (CTR), Nancy F. Castaldo; 139 (LO), Tina Manley/AL; 140 (UP LE), dpa picture alliance/AL; 140 (UP RT), Jake Lyell/AL; 140 (CTR), Image Source/AL; 140 (LO), Philip Game/AL; 141 (UP), Sandy Huffaker/Corbis/GI; 141 (LO RT), Universal Images Group/GI; 142 (UP), Hcongthanh/DRMS; 142 (CTR), Yuri Smityuk/TASS/GI; 142 (LO LE), World Central Kitchen; 142 (LO RT), Tetiana Zbrodko/DRMS; 143 (UP), Tatsiana Hendzel/DRMS; 143 (LO), Stan Honda/AFP/GI

Back matter: 145 (CTR), Annegordon/DRMS; 154 (LO), Valentina Razumova/DRMS

159

Since 1888, the National Geographic Society has funded more than 12,000 research, exploration, and preservation projects around the world. The Society receives funds from National Geographic Partners, LLC, funded in part by your purchase. A portion of the proceeds from this book supports this vital work. To learn more, visit natgeo.com/info.

NATIONAL GEOGRAPHIC and Yellow Border Design are trademarks of the National Geographic Society, used under license.

For more information, visit nationalgeographic.com, call 1-877-873-6846, or write to the following address:

National Geographic Partners
1145 17th Street N.W.
Washington, D.C. 20036-4688 U.S.A.

Visit us online at nationalgeographic.com/books

For librarians and teachers: nationalgeographic.com/books/librarians-and-educators

More for kids from National Geographic: natgeokids.com

National Geographic Kids magazine inspires children to explore their world with fun yet educational articles on animals, science, nature, and more. Using fresh storytelling and amazing photography, *Nat Geo Kids* shows kids ages 6 to 14 the fascinating truth about the world—and why they should care. **kids.nationalgeographic.com/subscribe**

For rights or permissions inquiries, please contact National Geographic Books Subsidiary Rights: bookrights@natgeo.com

Editorial, Design, and Production by Bender Richardson White

National Geographic supports K–12 educators with ELA Common Core Resources. Visit natgeoed.org/commoncore for more information.

Acknowledgments: The publisher would like to thank the book team: Priyanka Lamichhane and Libby Romero, senior editors; Lori Epstein, photo director; Kathryn Robbins, senior designer; Alix Inchausti, production editor; Anne LeongSon and Gus Tello, design production assistants; and for Bender Richardson White: Lionel Bender, project manager; Ben White, art director; Kim Richardson, production manager; Nancy F. Castaldo and Christy Mihaly, writers; Lee Tran Lam, food consultant; Sharon Dortenzio, photo editor; Amron Gravett, indexer; Catherine Farley, copy editor and proofreader.

Trade paperback ISBN: 978-1-4263-3867-0
Reinforced library binding ISBN: 978-1-4263-3868-7

Printed in Hong Kong
20/PPHK/1